Writing to the Prompt

When Students Don't Have a Choice

Janet Angelillo

HEINEMANN
Portsmouth, NH

HEINEMANN
A division of Reed Elsevier Inc.
361 Hanover Street
Portsmouth, NH 03801–3912
www.heinemann.com

Offices and agents throughout the world

Library of Congress Cataloging-in-Publication Data
Angelillo, Janet.
    Writing to the prompt : when students don't have a choice / Janet Angelillo.
        p. cm.
    Includes bibliographical references and index.
    ISBN 0-325-00759-4 (alk. paper)
    1. English language—Composition and exercises—Study and teaching
(Elementary).   2. Report writing—Study and teaching (Elementary).
3. Language arts (Elementary).   I. Title.

LB1576.A626   2005
372.62'3—dc22   2005016360

Editor: Kate Montgomery
Production editor: Sonja S. Chapman
Cover design: Lisa Fowler
Compositor: Technologies 'N Typography
Manufacturing: Jamie Carter

Printed in the United States of America on acid-free paper
09   08   07   06   RRD   2   3   4   5

In memory of my parents,
Mary and Jerry

Contents

Introduction 1

Chapter 1   Writing Workshop
The Foundation of Writing Instruction 5

Chapter 2   Video Game Thinking, or Finding an Analogy 12

Chapter 3   Talk Among Yourselves
The Role of Conversation in Responding to Prompts 19

Chapter 4   Intellectual Play
Digging into Others' Ideas. 28

Chapter 5   The Daily Work
Using Prompts to Lift the Level of Student Work 50

Chapter 6   What About Your Rights?
Assigned Topics for Content-Area Work 76

Chapter 7   The Writer's Job
Assigned Topics and the Qualities of Good Writing. 100

Chapter 8   Living with an Idea
Units of Study for Writing About Assigned Topics 115

Chapter 9   Write About This
Preparing Students for Timed Writing on Demand 132

Chapter 10   How'd It Go?
Assessing Writing About Assigned Topics. 144

Concluding Thoughts 154

References 156

Index 163

Acknowledgments

I have mused on this topic with so many folks over the past few years, and I cannot remember them all. But I would like to thank everyone, including the nameless kind souls in coffee shops, young people at arcades, and teachers all over the United States and Canada who listened to me.

Many thanks to my friends for their love and support: Carol Bogen, Meredith Downey, Margot Ward, Janet and John Hough, Avis Sri-Jayantha, Jane Berger, Deb Donaldson and John Wehr, Phoebe Cottingham, Karen Holtslag, Susan Goodman, Jill Sitkin, Charlotte Nganele, Connie Douglas, Susan and Gordon Smith. I lean on you more than you know.

Thanks to my dear colleagues Carl Anderson, Shirley McPhillips, Katie Wood Ray, Katherine Bomer, Laura Robb, Ruth Culham, Lucy Calkins, Isoke Nia, Randy Bomer. Your voices are always in my ears.

To my wonderful editor and friend, Kate Montgomery, and the editorial and production staffs at Heinemann—thanks for your patience and professionalism. Kate, you help me to believe in the impossible.

My precious family: Charles, Mark, Cheryl, and Alex and the tribe. You love me even when I'm attached to the computer.

Thanks to the teachers and principals who made this book possible: Sarah Daunis, Adele Schroeter, Mary Ellyn Lehner, Abby Devaney, Stephanie Rypka, Erik Perotti, Patrick Allen, Laura Hayes, Beth Dropick, Tina Colangelo, Cheryl Dwyer, Rebecca Mikus, Mary Beth Crupi, Liz Guhl, Vicky Cavanaugh, Laura Carlson, Rose Chodos, Jane Cooke, Sally Dodd, Kerry D'Angelo, Karen Nagy, Patricia Schultz, Leslie Pearson, Ed Wachowski, Susan Proto, Anmarie Galgano, Barbara Halzel, Jane Levy.

And to students everywhere who greet me with warmth and openness to hear my story again and again. May you all be writers.

Introduction

I grew up in postwar New York, in a large outer-borough enclave where everyone knew everyone else. Until my sister was born, I was an only child among many adults—my parents, two sets of grandparents, and numerous single aunts and uncles. We all lived in the same small house, eating, talking, playing, arguing. But now, when I go back to visit that house, it is quiet and almost empty.

In the last decade, as I realized all my dear relatives were nearing the end of their lives, I began to scribble down their stories: fleeing earthquakes and cholera in Europe; living in cold-water flats; using outdoor privies behind tenement buildings; cooking by gaslight, warming cold feet on the kitchen coal stove; and, of course, living with remnants of war memories—rationing, dark shades, empty streets, night sirens, choking fear. I also recorded the sanitized war stories my father told me so that I would eat my vegetables when I was young. The stories were about cooking pasta in his helmet, about trekking through India and Burma as a radio operator, about following mules because he knew they could find water in the jungle, and so on. I knew I had to get those stories on paper, and now my writer's notebook is full of them. In many ways, writing about my family's history mirrors a writing workshop: It was meaningful, self-selected, self-chosen, self-motivated, lifelong writing. That notebook is the full house of the love, laughter, and lives I knew.

Finally, time took its toll. All but one of these elder relatives has passed on—one by one, the generation that knew the Italian diaspora, the Depression, and World War II has been lost to age and disease. The only remaining relative is the eldest aunt, Francesca, our "Aunt Fran" who at ninety-two lives alone in the house once filled with company, cooking, and conversation. When the last uncle died, independent Aunt Fran finally admitted she needed help, so she engaged a lawyer to name my sister and me as her health care proxies.

Here begins my story of assigned topics. While I recorded the stories of our family because I wanted them safely kept in my notebooks, they were born of my own need. No one assigned me the task, except that I knew the clock was ticking on a generation I loved and would miss terribly. But suddenly, a huge amount of the writing for my family—my lone aunt—was not the self-directed recording of family stories; it was writing that would literally keep my aunt alive.

I confess that, up until then, I didn't realize how much of my writing *is* assigned. Yes, I keep a writer's notebook (Murray, 1985; Calkins, 1994; Fletcher, 1996). I write in hotel rooms, at airports, on trains, at home, in the car, or in waiting rooms—always writing, writing, writing, using my scribbles to figure out who I am, what I think, and what I want to say. Most often I write for myself. I have no papers to do for school anymore, other than lesson plans and occasional letters . . . so therefore, I have no assignments. Or so I once thought.

The process of taking over responsibility for my aunt's health suddenly required lots of assignments: letters and statements, written explanations of who I was to every doctor my aunt sees and the reasons I was dismissing some of them, lists of required medicines for the home care helper, lengthy complaint letters about inaccurate billing, instructions to those who maintain the house, letters to social agencies, and so on. I continued to write notebook entries and poetry in hotels and at airports, but I had more writing to do for what my aunt needed. I was writing documents that were critical to the health and survival of an elderly person who was now completely dependent on me. And one night, in a flash, I saw this as *assigned writing*. It was assigned because it was not my choice of topic or genre, and because I was taking on my aunt's ideas and issues and writing about them. For me, this was an entirely new perspective on writing. I thought it had the burden of work about it, because it involved the care of an invalid's life and the ghostly emptiness of old age. But it was completely necessary. More and more, as I wrote on her behalf, I began to see returns on my writing investment, *and* I saw her smile.

More than lovely life stories in my notebook, this writing matters in real ways. In the world, it gets me what I need and want, like getting Aunt Fran excused from jury duty, prescriptions delivered to her house, and her health insurance renewed. Far from being burdensome, the writing is rewarding. It brings results; court officers respond, doctors write back, new insurance cards are delivered. The effects are enormous, though teachers tend to value personal stories more. This paradox is surprising to me.

How much of one's life writing is assigned? And how does this affect what teachers teach and how they teach it? In recent decades, the focus in writing workshops has shifted toward authentic writing experiences, and students now learn a process for writing that emphasizes the thinking behind a writer's work. They also learn about writing in real-world genres and about finding topics from their lives so that they write about things that very much matter to them. This change in the teaching of writing is significant, and for many students, writing has finally come alive as a means of self-expression and as a way to validate thinking and establish voice. Many students now know how to find ideas for writing without a teacher's prompting and to develop ideas, plan the writing, create drafts, revise and edit, and produce published or final products.

However, while turning toward teaching students to manage their writing lives and their learning, teachers have overlooked an important fact. The truth is that much student writing in school, and in the real world after graduation, is not from self-generated topics but in response to assigned topics. Whether in content-area and literature classes or on high school entrance essays and statewide writing assessments, assigned topics are a pervasive reality of school life. In the world beyond school, much real-world writing is also for assigned topics. It arises from the circumstances of everyone's lives and grows from the necessity of writing for *others* rather than for ourselves. This writing is required by modern life: job or college applications, work-related reports, licensing examinations, eulogies, toasts, presentations to clients or to the school board, complaint or thank-you letters, directions and lists, and so on. It's the majority of the writing in people's lives, whether or not they compose poems or love letters in private moments.

This is not to imply that the work of those writers' workshops is not important—no, it is probably the most important work students will ever do in school, for themselves and for humanity. But it seems fair to say that in the well-intentioned zeal for teaching students to write from self-generated topics about their own lives, teachers have forgotten that often they can't do that. The challenge, therefore, is to teach them all the qualities of good writing through the topics that matter to them, and then to teach them to transfer those qualities to writing for assigned topics. Students must be taught to become engaged with another person's ideas, much the same way as they do when playing video games, and to become interested in assigned topics even though they are not self-generated. Teachers must show them how thinkers position themselves to *be* interested in intellectual play because they have the thinking and writing tools for doing so. In fact, being interested in others' ideas and building the capacity to play with or dig into them is critical to supporting understanding across cultures, races, and religions. It creates habits of mind that respect and honor beliefs and ideas that are different; it creates expansive thinking that seeks to explore others' ideas rather than egocentrically dismissing them. As Nikki Giovanni said: "Writers write from empathy" (1994, 106). Writing about the thoughts and ideas of others involves compassion and empathy.

When teaching students to write well to self-generated topics and then to transfer their thinking to assigned topics, teachers teach them a life skill they will use again and again. While the hope is that they will continue to write self-generated poetry and stories, teachers must be sure that they can write in response to questions and needs. All the poetry I write on airplanes does nothing to get my aunt the medication she needs or the plumber to her house (though it helps me to deal with the situation). And while I need to write poetry for myself, I also need to write in response to others' needs. My personal writing is the expression of the deep yearnings of my soul—its sorrows, regrets, reminiscences, joys, loves, passions. My writing in response to prompts helps me grasp and deal with the world—its bureaucracy and beauty, its indifference and innocence, its opposition and opportunity. In many ways, it is exciting to interact with others' ideas as I think and write. It keeps me from cocooning with my own thoughts and makes me wiser, compassionate, and open-minded.

This book examines writing workshop as a way to teach the thinking behind writing and offers teachers practical ways to scaffold their students' thinking and writing to prepare for assigned writing topics. It is meant to show teachers that, in the end, writing from one's life is not very different from writing on assignment and that, ethically, teachers must teach children to do both. The challenge is to send young writers into the world able to write from their own hearts and passions, as well as to the queries and challenges of others. Much the same as students write well when they care about their topics, to build a better world, those who teach must help them care about others' ideas. To build a better world for my aunt, I care about her needs and ideas. To build a better global world, I must care about needs and ideas five thousand miles away from me.

Engaging with others' thinking is not drudgery, but a way to human understanding and, possibly, to world peace. The demands of this global society require everyone to have the ability to engage with others' thinking to build social justice and peace for all humanity. Teaching writing to prompts within writing workshop may be one way to accomplish this.

Writing Workshop

The Foundation of Good Writing Instruction

It is an early September morning with humid dew covering the trees, grass, and cars, and the promise that the wet chill will give way to afternoon warmth. I look forward to the new school year with both joy and anxiety, as I have every year since I was a little girl. I still can't sleep the night before the first day of school because the culture of school that seems so familiar in June is fraught with uncertainty by September. I am jumpy as I climb the school steps.

On this first morning, I enter a school to work with teachers on launching writing workshop and setting acceptable standards for student writing. Their assistant principal, Mary Beth Crupi, supports them in many ways, including participating in study groups and teaching alongside them. They are a professional learning community (DuFour and Eaker, 1998; Sergiovanni, 1994), but as soon as I walk in the room, I sense their tension and unease. "It's the test," one teacher tells me, as the others nod, "we feel responsible for students to do well on the test."

The tests. Students take so many tests these days that it is difficult not to see them as the centerpoint of the teaching year. Many teachers feel compelled to spend much of the instructional time on practicing for tests. In some cases, students grind away at practice answers to testlike writing prompts from early September until the tests' dates. In all likelihood, state and local assessments will grow in number because so much is riding on them, from district reputations, to money allocations, to property values. For these reasons, teachers will do well to take state and local tests seriously, though I believe that good teaching all year long prepares students for test-taking.

Just as important are the innumerable times students write to prompts apart from state tests: those science and lab reports and social studies tests, the ever-present winter biography about a famous person, and so on. Writing to teachers' prompts is a reality for most students in many schools; in some schools, it is the only writing students do. Even in schools where some teachers have moved to student choice of topics in language arts classes, writing to prompts persists in other content areas. The only process writing is that done in writing workshop. What a missed opportunity to marry the two for the best results—writing that is meaningful and well-written.

Self-selection of topics and writing to assignment are not mutually exclusive. The purpose of teaching writing is so that students can write well all the time. What is neglected is teaching students *how* to carry over their learning from times when they are writing about topics of their choice to opportunities for using those skills with someone else's topic. Teachers' work not only must be teaching writing well but also teaching students how to engage with others' ideas, to make them their own and write well about them. It takes more teaching to do this than to assign topics every week for "practice." Furthermore, engaging with others' ideas is an essential life skill. As I wrote in this book's introduction, all their lives students will write to prompts in school, at work, in life.

What exactly does it mean to write to a prompt? *Prompt writing* means listening to or reading someone's idea or question, thinking about it, and responding. Often there are other variables the writer must negotiate, such as time constraints, needing to answer several parts or sections, measuring the writing against a rubric of requirements, and making necessary adjustments in corrections. One of the biggest variables is whether writing to the prompt is to be done alone or after the writer is able to talk with peers about the writing. In many situations, student writers are writing solo and cannot test their ideas with others before writing. In some cases, huge consequences, such as admission to college or specialized high schools, ride on the writing event. In all cases, students must have the capacity to comprehend what is required and to think and write to respond completely. It is a complex process that goes far beyond using writing formulas. Students must determine not only what the question asks but also the type of response required (e.g., narrative, expository, list). Differing situations, such as time variables, present different challenges for the writer. This is not an easy task for the novice writer, nor even the experienced one.

In addition, prompt thinking and prompt writing are important in a larger sense. Living in the world involves engaging with others' ideas, churning them in one's mind and through discussion, and creating new thinking, whether responding to the news, a friend's or colleague's thinking, or an uncle's political rantings at a holiday dinner. Students must learn to respect their own ideas and know how to engage with those of others as well. I advocate strong, vital writing workshops where students learn to discover and write about topics that matter to them. Once they understand that writing is gratifying, students can be taught to take on each other's and the teacher's ideas. This involves the "brain work" of constructing knowledge from an outside idea, question, or hypothesis.

This chapter takes a look at the basics of how to teach writing to assigned topics and examines the structure of writing workshop and how writing workshop supports writing to prompts.

The Structure of Writing Workshop

Before considering how to teach students to write well to assigned topics, it is essential to establish a literacy community that focuses on teaching students to write well for any occasion. One of the most effective ways to do this is to teach within the writing workshop model (Murray, 1985; Graves, 1989; Calkins, 1994; Fletcher, 1992; Davis and Hill, 2003; Ray, 1999). I consider the writing workshop essential to the teaching of writing and especially to teaching prompt writing. Writing workshop instruction is intense and multilayered, and it leads to sophisticated and insightful writing. It focuses on the *process* of writing, although the concept of a "process" in reality describes all complex behaviors (Tobin, 1994).

In writing workshop, teachers assess students' writing needs and design whole-class, small-group, and individual instruction that supports student learning (Anderson, 2005; Calkins, Hartman, and White, 2005). This model sets rigorous standards for student writing, both in amount and quality. The underlying philosophy is that students will learn best when they construct their own learning (Bruner, 1966; Vygotsky, 1986), and they will learn to write well if they are invested in their writing (Graves, 1989; Calkins, 1994; Murray, 1985).

The workshop model thrives on ongoing, continuous learning and inquiry, and the belief that learning never ends. Therefore, students become accustomed to intellectual play and to continually reworking and revising their ideas (Angelillo, 2005). They learn to make informed choices about their work and to self-assess and plan for further learning under the teacher's guidance (see Figure 1–1). With these factors in place, the

- Establishing a literate community where everyone, including the teacher, is learning more and more about writing (Peterson, 1992; Ray, 1999).

- Teaching focused on "teaching the writer, not the writing" (Murray, 1985; Calkins, 1994)—that is, teaching writing strategies students can use in any piece of writing.

- Writing instruction based on the "process of writing" (Flower and Hayes, 1980, 1981; Calkins, 1994). Writers "live" expecting to collect ideas for writing; they develop some of those ideas by researching, collecting words, freewriting, and so on; they write first drafts and they revise (Angelillo, 2005); they edit and proofread; and they send their finished writing into the community expecting that it will be read by others.

- Teaching centers on writing strategies through modeling or demonstrating—in short, concise, carefully planned minilessons that each last 10 to 15 minutes; demonstrations are done with the teacher's own writing, a student's writing, or by examining literature.

- Teaching is organized into units of study throughout the year, including some genre studies (e.g., memoir, poetry, essay) and some nongenre studies (e.g., written conventions, revision, independence).

- Writing every day for a specified amount of time; this time expands to as much as forty-five minutes to one hour as students develop stamina for writing.

- Giving students choices (e.g., topic, ways to develop ideas, revision strategies); however, within the choices is the responsibility to engage thoroughly with topics, practice writing strategies, and publish regularly.

FIG. 1–1 *Some basic cornerstones for writing workshops*

teacher can begin to work with students on taking their writing skills and transferring them to prompt writing, which becomes part of the intellectual work of the classroom.

Writing workshops are both highly structured and sophisticated, though little or none of the writing is to prompts. Choice of topic and often of genre are important for the development of fledgling writers. Instruction focuses on writing strategies and acknowledges that all students do not progress the same in the process of writing; thus, they often make decisions about writing and writing strategies (Schneider, 1997). Through effective teaching in writing workshop, students learn the strategies to write on assignment as well as to their own topics. However, some teachers worry that students don't know how to transfer writing strategies from workshops to writing on assignment; that is what this book is about to demonstrate.

I believe that productive writing workshops must precede the teaching of prompt writing, because workshop teaching is the basis for learning to engage with topics and to use writing strategies to expand and revise students' writing. A good writing workshop contains all the elements of good teaching and good writing, as well as facilitates students' understanding that writing is not just completing assignments to satisfy the teacher. It is learning to think, to make decisions, and to affect others with one's writing. What better preparation for writing to prompts?

All this is important because it demonstrates that teaching writing is a deliberate, ongoing, serious affair. When attempting to teach students to write well to assigned topics, teachers must first consider whether they have actually taught them to write well. In writing workshop, almost every day is spent learning new strategies for writing, including expanding ideas, using words carefully, crafting sentences, using grammar and punctuation effectively, revising thoughtfully, considering audience, writing with voice and conviction (Ray, 1999; Culham, 2003; Fletcher and Portalupi, 2001; Romano, 2004; see sidebar too). Such qualities belong in any well-written piece.

Teachers also need to scaffold student learning by shaping students' cognitive processes through verbal interaction with expert models (Vygotsky, 1978; Wertsch, 1984)—for example, the teacher's own processing of responses to prompts or those of written exemplars. So often though, well-meaning teachers hope students will get better at prompt writing by simply writing to a different prompt every day. In writing workshop, teaching should focus on good writing in any genre. The challenge is to teach writing well, and then teach students to transfer that learning to situations where they do not have the same amount of choice.

> **Important Books About Writing Workshop**
>
> - Anderson, Carl. 2000. *How's It Going?*
> - Anderson, Carl. 2005. *Assessing Writing*
> - Angelillo, Janet. 2005. *Making Revision Matter*
> - Angelillo, Janet. 2003. *A Fresh Approach to Teaching Punctuation*
> - Calkins, Lucy. 1994. *The Art of Teaching Writing, rev. ed.*
> - Calkins, Lucy, Amanda Hartman, and Zoe White. 2005. *One to One*
> - Culham, Ruth. 2003. *6 + 1 Traits of Writing*
> - Davis, Judy, and Sharon Hill. 2003. *The No-Nonsense Guide to Teaching Writing*
> - Fletcher, Ralph. 1992. *What a Writer Needs*
> - Fletcher, Ralph, and JoAnn Portalupi. 2001. *Writing Workshop: The Essential Guide*
> - Harwayne, Shelley. 1992. *Lasting Impressions*
> - Peterson, Ralph. 1992. *Life in a Crowded Place*
> - Robb, Laura. 2004. *Nonfiction Writing From the Inside Out*
> - Ray, Katie Wood. 2001. *The Writing Workshop: Working Through the Hard Parts (and They're All Hard Parts)*
> - Ray, Katie Wood. 1999. *Wondrous Words*

Writing Workshop Supports Writing to Prompts

Because writing workshops focus on strengthening writing strategies and thereby raise the bar for all writing, they are the perfect way to teach students to write well to prompts. When students learn to write strong beginnings, use specific words, or write about significant details, their writing improves. The challenge for the teacher is to help students transfer knowledge about writing strategies to prompt writing (see Table 1–1).

TABLE 1–1 Writing Workshop Supports Writing to Prompts

Writing Workshop	Writing to Prompts
Establishing a literate community where everyone, including the teacher, is learning more and more about writing (Peterson, 1992; Ray, 1999).	Establishing an inquiry-based community that studies how to intellectually engage with an idea.
Teaching focused on "teaching the writer, not the writing" (Murray, 1985; Calkins, 1994)—that is, teaching writing strategies students can use in any piece of writing.	Teaching focuses on writing strategies that cross all writing genres, including writing to prompts; the purpose is to teach the student to be a better writer in all cases.
Writing instruction based on the "process of writing" (Flower and Hayes, 1980, 1981; Calkins, 1994). Writers "live" expecting to collect ideas for writing; they develop some of those ideas by researching, collecting words, freewriting, and so on; they write first drafts and they revise (Angelillo, 2005); they edit and proofread; and they send their finished writing into the community expecting that it will be read by others.	Writers also use the writing process to write to prompts, including developing ideas, planning writing, drafting, revising, editing, and expecting that real audiences will read their writing.
Teaching centers on writing strategies through modeling or demonstrating—in short, concise, carefully planned minilessons that each last 10 to 15 minutes; demonstrations are done with the teacher's own writing, a student's writing, or by examining literature.	Teaching focuses on the intellectual engagement with another's idea by teachers' modeling of how to do this metacognitively; teachers demonstrate by thinking aloud and by using their own writing or exemplar student writing.
Teaching is organized into units of study throughout the year, including some genre studies (e.g., memoir, poetry, essay) and some nongenre studies (e.g., written conventions, revision, independence).	Teaching occurs throughout the year so that students learn the qualities of good writing, continue to engage with ideas, practice writing in notebooks, and complete a unit of study on writing to prompts.
Writing every day for a specified amount of time; this time expands to as much as forty-five minutes to one hour as students develop stamina for writing.	Students practice writing to prompts in increasing time increments.
Giving students choices (e.g., topic, ways to develop ideas, revision strategies); however, within the choices is the responsibility to engage thoroughly with topics, practice writing strategies, and publish regularly.	Students assign topics to each other for initial practice; when the teacher assigns a topic, they still have choices when developing the topic, planning, revising, and so on; students are expected to thoroughly engage with topics and to discuss ways to practice this.

Summary

Writing workshop is a sophisticated, respectful structure for teaching writing to students. It values them as learners and requires a belief that all students can and will learn to write if given proper and ongoing instruction, and a block of time to write every day. Although one of the foundations of writing workshop is the opportunity for students to choose their own topics, it also provides the best structure for teaching them to write to prompts. Prompt writing should occur within the supportive environment of the writing workshop rather than outside and apart from it.

To Do in Classrooms

- Establish a plan for professional reading about writing workshops

- Set aside time every day to write

- Become a writer—the best writing lessons will come from your own attempts at writing

- Use your writing to teach writing strategies

- Begin a study group with other teachers on writing workshop's aspects (e.g., keeping a writer's notebook, revision, using literature to teach writing)

2

Video Game Thinking, or Finding an Analogy

My son Mark is a "gamer." He tells me that is correct language for "one who plays video games" *all* the time. I recall the ongoing tiffs he and I had when he was in middle and high school because I wanted him to read the classics, and he just wanted to play video games. He eventually read many of those classics—when his interest in Dostoyevsky and Henry James was sparked in college and he could understand the content with an adult mind. But the video games also stayed with him; he in fact now makes his living from computers. So who was right? Of course, the answer is both of us.

There is no doubt that reading is critical to developing thinking skills and to considering the universality of the human condition, not to mention one's employability. But today, video games have produced a generation that has a new set of skills to bring to their learning. For example, some doctors are now experimenting with using gaming to sharpen their motor skills, reaction time, and hand–eye coordination as preparation for doing laparoscopic surgery (Dobnik, 2004). There is some evidence that gamers have improved spatial visualization skills and scientific and mathematical aptitude (Lowery and Knirk, 1982). Perhaps this is the start of a new era of academic acceptance of video games as some of the benefits of them are acknowledged (Carlson, 2002). Certainly there are elements in some video games that many question, such as graphic violence and brutal competition, though those are not examined in this book. But there are other elements teachers can tap into to help students think about and eventually write to prompts. Therefore, this chapter examines the use of gaming analogies to teach complex thinking skills and of classroom activities to support analogic thinking.

Using Gaming Analogies to Teach Complex Thinking Skills

Successfully playing video games requires a complex set of strategies (Nawrocki and Winner, 1983). Many games require sustained player attention and sharp intelligence, and many have layered contextual meanings, including literary allusions, archetypal characters, and ancient or mythical symbols. Players must choose between numerous options in a game, often requiring immediate response and knowledge of other games. Also, there are many types of games—those that contain sophisticated narratives in which the player participates in a quest of some difficulty and duration; those with simulation and adventure, which may help to develop strategic thinking and planning skills; sports games, which offer the virtual experience of playing everything from football to golf—not unlike the virtual technology that lets doctors determine where to operate via TV screens and probes; "first-person shooter" (FPS) games in which the player advances through levels of increasing difficulty while slaying demons and the like.

The games are often compelling and young players can "get lost" in them, the way many adults remember getting lost in books when they were young. This is not to say that there is a dichotomy between book reading and gaming but to establish that some of the same experiences provided by books can also occur in well-written games. Studies have shown that nearly 77 percent of adolescents play video games daily (Phillips, 1995). Although I would rather cozy up with a good book than to some kind of screen, I acknowledge that video games are here to stay, at least until a newer technological invention makes them obsolete. In fact, as I write this, interactive video games that require dancing are becoming the rage.

For those who are not video game savvy (like myself), let's imagine other types of games that require complete engagement. Some teachers play sports or board games, others are musicians or artists. Some like puzzles or word games. When thinking about whether any of these is an analogy for prompt writing, it is clear that they all provide teachers with ways to connect to students' thinking. If it is not comfortable to use the video game analogy, any game analogy probably will do. Anyone who has had the experience of "becoming the game" can understand getting lost in intellectual play. Even with the physical exercise of sports, engagement with the rules and quick decision-making skills are required.

For the purposes of teachers' work with prompts, playing video games, or using any of the previously mentioned game activities, is like taking on assigned topics. The creators of a game invent a scenario or establish a set of rules. To succeed, players must be willing to enter into that scenario or to engage with those rules. Before they can proceed, players must understand what is required. Generally, they need to assess the task and the powers of the enemies encountered, meet and overcome obstacles, make decisions by accepting or rejecting possible solutions, decide on a persona to take on or a mission, and/or decide on a level of difficulty for the game. Most of these skills are needed to write well to prompts; however, notice two differences: (1) most video games give immediate and high-quality feedback and (2) they usually allow graceful recovery from mistakes. Teachers must be imaginative about ways to build these two elements into instruction.

Of course, some elements of video games cannot be reproduced in regular classroom instruction: gorgeous graphics, action, danger, music and sound effects, competition, and becoming one with the game. But some video game elements and resultant skills can be used, including those listed in the sidebar.

If one examines this list, it appears that some behaviors are solitary acts and others are best done with partners or a group, just as some video games are solitary and others are group endeavors. Much of this work can be rehearsed through talking with others (see Chapter 3). In all cases, by demonstrating thinking—making it visible—teachers can show students exactly what they mean in relation to responding to any topic in terms of "gaming" it. The main purpose is to recognize that students develop these skills on their own through playing games and that they can be taught to transfer those skills to writing.

Let's imagine taking on one of the topics I've seen in one district: "You go into your grandmother's attic and find a trunk. You open it. Write about what you find inside." By thinking aloud a teacher can demonstrate ways to use gaming strategies to think and write about a topic (see Table 2–1). Such a gaming analogy might involve video games, but feel free to use whatever analogy feels comfortable. Most game situations will fit the thinking strategies and can be used as analogies. The important point is to find some analogy students can relate to and to use it to build their thinking about prompts.

TABLE 2–1 Use Gaming Strategies for Thinking and Writing

Game Thinking Strategies	Think-alouds to Apply Game Thinking to Writing About a Topic
• Being ready to engage with a topic as an intellectual exercise	"I don't have a grandmother or she doesn't have an attic, but I will go along with this idea by thinking about movies or TV shows I've seen with grandmothers and attics; I can take on any grandmother or attic as my own." "I also try to imagine what a trunk looks like, even if I'm not sure. I guess that I can make it big or small as long as there is something inside." "Even if I'm not excited about the prompt or the situation in a game, I allow myself to follow it through. I pretend to be a good sport." "I think that this can be fun and I can do it." "What will I learn from trying it?" "How will I feel as I try this on, even though it may feel strange or new to me?"
• Being alert and quick to respond	"I figure out how to get myself interested in the topic, even if it's to make some sketches or notes to jar my thinking." "I decide I can't cop out and say the trunk is empty."
• Searching the mind to bring knowledge and information forward; that is, activating prior knowledge	"I think of friends or neighbors who have grandmothers or attics, or of stories I've heard about them." "I think about adult talk I've overheard about grandmothers or attics." "I use anything as my own."
• Considering many possibilities, selecting some and discarding others	"I decide not to use the creepy attic story I heard or the sad one about a grandmother dying." "I catalog the stories in my mind to see which one will get me to the trunk quickly and I go with that one." "It's the one I heard about how my friend's aunt saves everything—I'm going to use her as my grandmother and put everything in her trunk."
• Deciding on the type of game or response needed	"They don't want to know about the attic or the grandmother, so I just have to make the stuff in the trunk interesting or imaginative." "I decide they want a personal narrative or story about opening a trunk, not a feature article on trunks or an editorial on grandmothers." "I see that I have two pages to fill for the answer, so I need to plan some details to include."

TABLE 2–1 Use Gaming Strategies for Thinking and Writing (continued)

Game Thinking Strategies	Think-alouds to Apply Game Thinking to Writing About a Topic
• Revising as necessary, often starting over or changing strategy quickly	"I revise my plan before I write." "If there is time, I revise the draft of my writing." "I check against the question to be sure I answered it."
• Working collaboratively, especially for games with many players, whenever appropriate	"By talking through possible responses with a partner or small group, I am able to get feedback on the strength of my response and the reward of my peers' encouragement." (*Note:* Teachers should "listen in" to students' conversation and give immediate feedback as well.) "I work with a trusted partner to help me formulate a plan for response, and I help my partner do the same." "I share my strategies and hunches with others to get their feedback."
• Meeting and overcoming obstacles	"I have one or two ideas for how to answer, but not enough. So I go back to the planning page and do more sketching, webbing, listing, and so on." "I pull something out of the box and then I'm not sure how to write about it, so I have to visualize it, imagine touching and smelling it, and so on."
• Determining the degree of difficulty of a task and/ or the amount and type of energy required	"I make a decision about whether a short, quick answer is expected, or whether I have to write a full page with many details. In both cases, I plan for the task."
• Putting oneself into the game; that is, creating a sense of oneness with the idea	"I imagine myself inside the prompt, and I make the idea matter very much to me by caring about the outcome." "I mentally engage the idea enough so that I have a spin or a slant on it—the way I suspect certain characters to be enemies in video games and I treat them accordingly." "I allow myself to get lost in the idea, as if it is all I can think about for a time."
• Becoming intrigued by what will happen	"I step back and watch myself think of possible solutions or do some writing because I am curious to see what my brain will figure out about the prompt."

It is impossible to demonstrate all the thinking strategies described in the table at one time, but this shows that work could be spread across time to build student skills for engaging with someone else's idea. The important point is to use what students may already know—from video gaming, sports, board games, and the like—and to use those thinking skills to teach how to transfer them to prompt writing.

Using Classroom Activities to Support Analogic Thinking

One way to teach game thinking might be to gather students into groups to talk about the skills they use for certain games. Begin by making a chart of all the types of games students like to play, keeping it to general games (e.g., basketball) rather than specific games (e.g., Monopoly). Choose five or six game topics and then ask students to choose which group they would like to join. Some students may not want to join any of those selected, but ask them to remember that part of gaming is learning to play other games. Still, try to let them join groups that closely fit their interests because the purpose is to draw on their knowledge of game playing as an analogy for thinking and writing. Once students are in the groups, demonstrate with the game the kinds of skills students should talk about. For example, less time should be spent on the great play a student made than on how he or she figured out what to do.

The purpose of this group discussion is for students to *name* how and what they think while they are playing a game. Much of what they say will mirror the list of strategies in Table 2–1, but often students describe their thinking with originality and insight. For example, one sixth grader told me that he "flies" into board games and imagines the board as a three-dimensional structure all around him. His teacher and I asked him to use that strategy when thinking about prompt writing—in effect, getting himself inside the question and seeing it all around him.

As students work with game analogies, they see that prompt writing is another type of game. True, it is not one most of them would choose to play, but it still is a game. Someone else creates the topic, someone else decides the rules. To participate, everyone must understand and agree to the rules. There are ways to "win"—write a good response—and ways that do not work. The best thinkers get themselves involved in the game scenario and enjoy the experience.

Let students play with game analogies and apply them to several games. Ask them to think about the analogies while on the school bus or in the gym. Have them write in their writing notebooks about their game skills, and talk to each other about which skills they use. While doing this, teachers set students up for engaging with prompts in new and exciting ways.

Summary

Writing workshop provides the best atmosphere for teaching writing. When teachers establish effective writing workshops, they provide students with ownership of learning and many strategies for writing well for any occasion. The first step to writing well to prompts is to talk about them and to model, by using think-alouds, the thought processes he or she uses to figure out how and what to respond. Rather than teaching skills that seem completely academic and foreign to students, teachers can tap into skills, such as video gaming or playing sports, they develop outside of school. This provides students with familiar models for thorough thinking about ideas and for finding ways to invent responses.

To Do in Classrooms

- Establish a rigorous writing workshop

- Use think-alouds to model and name your own thinking processes as you build an analogy in the room; write this on a chart to display

- Use skills students develop outside of school as a basis for thinking about prompt writing

- Establish short-term groups where students discuss game thinking and how it applies to their thinking about a topic

3

Talk Among Yourselves

The Role of Conversation in Responding to Prompts

I n many ways having a conversation is like responding to an assigned topic. Someone meets you in the supermarket and asks how your father is doing and you are expected to answer in more or less detail. If you are in a rush, you'll answer, "Better, thanks," and move on; if you have time, you may elaborate on his various doctor visits and how new medications are helping him. In either case, you are responding by talking to someone else's idea. The dinner party query—"So what do you do for fun?"—can either lead you to chat about hang gliding or crocheting, or send you into anxious fits if you've been working too much—it's an assigned topic you may have difficulty answering!

There are some people, however, who just don't know how to carry on a good conversation. They don't take the bait, so to say. You can pummel them with questions or tell a story about yourself and nothing will get them talking. It's as if they have no interest in what you are saying or the topic you are "assigning" them. I worry about the social skills of such people, as well as their thinking skills.

Having conversations is a way to *work* an idea. The thinking in the air that a good conversation produces is not only enjoyable, but it sets the stage for good thinking in the head later on. Many people have had the experience of walking away from a confrontation and imagining what *should* have been said. Practicing conversational skills helps everyone develop a bank of things to say. It also gives people a chance to throw ideas around and to *stretch* them. Students who practice talking about ideas in small groups and with partners eventually can have conversations in their heads, and later on, alone when writing to a prompt. All this says is that conversation is one way to set the stage for thinking and writing to prompts.

This chapter examines a small portion of the research that supports the use of conversation as a thinking and teaching strategy to prepare for prompt writing. Working as partners and in small groups to expand the thinking behind assigned topics is a powerful scaffolding technique; the sections that follow describe the power of conversation as a thinking tool for negotiating meaning and how to teach powerful conversation techniques.

The Power of Conversation as a Thinking Tool

Linda Flower notes that discourse is a "political act; it depends on reading a situation and reading the audience as well as reading texts and having good ideas. . . . It depends on savvy and critical intelligence, selecting the details and cues that matter, organizing and connecting information or, more accurately, transforming it into a plan for future use" (1994, 6). Teaching students to have conversations not only supports their social lives but also is critical to helping them develop intellectually. The exchange of ideas, and revising, adding, and changing them does more to teach students how to think than any rote activities. In fact, many educators have long advocated the use of talking as a way to construct knowledge and clarify thinking (Graves, 1989; Newkirk and McClure, 1992).

During conversations, students hear others' ideas and work through or *try out* their ideas. In many ways, talking leads to clarification of thinking and rehearsal for writing. Talking teaches students to plan what to say, say it, revise thinking, plan again, and so on. Speakers often finish saying one thing while they are planning the next. Giving students time to talk, process, and plan helps them stretch ideas and collect evidence for their writing. According to James Britton: "Language is a highly organized, systematic means of representing experience, and as such it assists us to organize all other ways of representing" (1993, 21). Gordon Wells notes that students' conversation is not only critical for their learning, but for teachers' understanding of how and what to teach them. Listening to conversations gives clues about how students are thinking and learning. Specifically, Wells says: "Language provides a means for reflecting on action . . . helping to establish connections between different aspects of . . . experience, using the power of language . . . to represent objects and events that are absent or no more than hypothetical possibilities" (1986, 111).

This is just what teachers want students to do when they respond to prompts, isn't it? They should use language to represent objects and events that are absent or no more than hypothetical possibilities. It is easy to appreciate how difficult it is for students to "get their minds around" prompts if they're considered in that light. The following are some of the types of prompts students might meet on tests.

- "If you were Abraham Lincoln, what would you have done?" (hypothetical possibility and absent event)

- "You find a trunk in your grandmother's attic. You open it. What do you find inside?" (absent object and hypothetical because maybe the student's grandmother lives in an apartment, another country, or is deceased)

- "What was going through Gilly's mind?" (hypothetical possibility—is it ever really possible to know what's in someone's mind?)

Such prompts demonstrate how difficult the task of writing to prompts can be for some students, especially when the prompts do not specify either an audience or the reasons for the writing task, or if the task does not seem realistic to young writers (Farr and Beck, 2003). Teachers understand why students might be given any of the preceding prompts—examiners want to evaluate students' creativity, ability to infer from and to understand events of another time period, and so on. Furthermore, the task is different when students are writing to a prompt within a time constraint rather than having multiple days to plan, draft, revise, and edit their work (Murray, 1985). However, I am suggesting that in order to answer any questions satisfactorily, one needs practice using language to make the abstract concrete. This language processing begins with conversations that teach students to practice the taking on of another's idea; language is the tool by which a question or idea is *kneaded* to arrive at an answer or insight. As Wells notes, "exploratory talk" is the key (1986).

Many researchers have concluded that language is a form of thought (McNeil, 1975; Lindsay and Norman, 1977) and a mediator of cognition (Anderson, 1995). Language is the way learners mediate complex skills toward levels of automaticity (Sokolov, 1972), and learners frequently use words to rehearse skills (Fitts, 1964; Meichenbaum, 1977). Eventually learners use inner or covert speech for tasks such as reading and problem solving (Bem, 1971), both of which comprise writing to prompts. Vygotsky (1962) says that the change from overt to inner speech is a different type of cognition in purpose and content. John C. Bean asserts that "one of the best ways to coach critical thinking—and to promote the kind of productive talk that leads to thoughtful and elaborated writing—is goal-directed use of [the] small group" (2001, 149). The question is how teachers use this information to plan teaching and writing.

Understanding how to write to prompts begins with thinking and talking about prompts. As students learn to have conversations and to engage their thinking with an external idea (i.e., an idea that originated with someone else), they learn strategies for dealing with prompts. Furthermore, they are making their "gaming" skills visible and applying them to academic ideas. Students' verbal interactions in small groups improves learning and increases the level of thinking (Golub et al., 1988; Johnson, Maruyama, Johnson, Nelson, and Skon, 1981). The powerful effect of talking when working with peers forces learners to critically analyze and restructure information (Bargh and Schul, 1980). When teachers plan instruction that involves student autonomy and interaction with writing, it has a productive effect on student thinking, which Hillocks (1986) refers to as the "environmental mode of instruction." Small-group conversations that focus on prompt writing can also affect their thinking as students build knowledge together.

Quite simply, students can be put together in small groups and asked to talk about assigned topics using some of their gaming skills. This way of applying their knowledge to a new task can give some students a "way in" to thinking about topics that often are too far from their experience to seem relevant. Their video and imaginative game-playing skills do just this. Teachers need to help students bridge the gap by teaching talking skills to support their thinking.

Teaching Powerful Conversation Techniques

The best way to teach talking skills is to "fishbowl"—model conversations by pairing with another adult. Obviously, it makes sense to rehearse a conversation ahead of time and to be aware of exactly which strategies students should hear and notice. This modeling and subsequent debriefing shows ways to talk and how to handle an unfamiliar idea. All this leads to talking about an assigned topic before writing about it.

Laura Hayes teaches sixth grade and is concerned that her students' conversations peter out after a few minutes. In partnerships, they each say what they are thinking about the class read-aloud and then conclude they're done. So Laura and I decide to fishbowl a conversation about their book, *Bridge to Terabithia* by Katherine Paterson. Laura and I each choose something from the book to talk about and agree that we will push ourselves to talk for five minutes on each idea. We ask students to listen less to the content of our conversation and more to the ways we keep ourselves "chatting," support each other's talking, and try to come to new insights with each other's help.

After our conversation, students were asked to tell us what they noticed; here is what they listed on a chart.

- We start by restating what we are going to talk about.

- We each talk a little to clarify what we are thinking about the topic.

- We relate the topic to our own lives, or to people we know who have had similar or opposite experiences.

- We ask each other questions for clarification and for more information.

- We disagree politely, while trying to see the other's point of view.

- We stop to reconsider the topic a few times and summarize as we talk.

- We look at the text to find examples of what we are talking about.

- We encourage each other to say more by complimenting good ideas.

- We use conversational phrases (see Table 2–1) to move the communication along.

- We agree to think more about our topics and talk again.

Next, students were told to talk with partners about the same book for five minutes. They were offered five possible topics to discuss and asked to choose one. Students referred to the preceding class list, but we also noticed that some students quickly "ran out of steam." For some students, merely having a conversation is difficult because they are not used to the give-and-take of talking. This leads educators to believe that they must be taught ways to "push" themselves to say more without giving up too early (Calkins, 2001), as well as be provided with opportunities for talk in small groups and with partners.

Students who become skilled at conversation usually have more practice using language to express their thoughts as well as negotiating meaning with others and clarifying what they mean. Long before asking them to *write* about prompts, teach them how to *talk* about a prompt for a long time. Allow students to practice talking about assigned topics and assess what they need to help them expand and deepen their thinking. As Lucy Calkins notes: "The mark of a good book talk is that people are not just reporting on ideas they've already had; they are, instead, generating new ideas together" (2001, 14). This can be extended to all academic conversations, and probably to good social conversations as well. The purpose of talking about any prompt is to generate ideas together on how to personally engage with the idea and respond to it.

Creating Structures for Talking About Prompts

Today, teachers are quite pressed for time. There is much to teach and so little time to teach it all. It is tempting to skip the thinking and conversation work of writing to prompts and head straight into writing. But this only provides for the repetition of writing to prompts, accompanied by looking at errors at the evaluation stage. While there is no reason to suggest that practice is not beneficial, there is much to do before students practice writing.

One important structure for encouraging talk in classrooms is to set up informal partnerships. For "talk" partnerships students sit beside each other during read-aloud time, or during the teacher's minilesson, and process information together. They might sit with the same person every day or rotate partners. Many teachers begin the partnering early in the school year, and eventually make it more structured by assessing reading and writing abilities and pairing students accordingly into more or less permanent partnerships. When deciding on partners, it is important to realize that pairs do not necessarily need to be ability-based; some struggling students are in fact even better at conversation than fluent readers and writers.

While I want to emphasize that reading and writing workshops provide lots of opportunity for student choice in what to talk about, partnerships should be set up to begin to teach students to take on an idea. During read-alouds or the reading or writing minilesson, the teacher needs to give each student the chance to talk about something she or he is thinking about the text.

For example, Abby Devany is reading *Touching Spirit Bear* by Ben Mikaelson to her seventh-grade class. Many times she asks students to just turn and talk about their responses to the text, particularly after they have a solid idea about the book (Angelillo, 2003a; Calkins, 2001; Routman, 2000). Sometimes, however, she poses provocative questions or statements for them to discuss with partners. She goes around the room listening in to their conversations, both to hear their insights into the text and to hear how they are able to converse and grapple with an idea. After their talks, she asks them to record some of what they said in their readers' notebooks.

TABLE 3–1 Using Gaming Skills to Improve Thinking Skills

Gaming Skill	Thinking About Text
Think about what you already know about how games are played; use that to help you figure out the game. For example, you know there will be some kind of scoring or point system and some opposition.	Think about what you already know about how books go in general (e.g., the protagonist usually doesn't die early in the book, if at all); use that knowledge to help you make predictions.
Identify the type of game and plan how to play based on what you know about how such a game goes.	Use setting and genre to help you figure out what type of book this is, then make predictions based on those elements.
When you play a video game you aren't quite sure when the tide will turn. A new enemy may appear or someone may draw a powerful card in a board game. Be prepared to change directions and make decisions based on new developments.	Be ready to live with a little uncertainty, because the answers to some questions are not in the text. You have to infer them from what you see.
Think about the object of the game. If you are the main character in a video game, what is the challenge you face? In other games, what do you have to accomplish (e.g., score points, stop the other team)?	Think about what the challenge (e.g. to pinpoint and understand a character's emotions) is for you as a reader, and/or what the challenge is for the character.
Identify the emotions—excitement, fear, suspense, frustration, exultation—you feel while playing the game.	Put yourself into the situation (e.g., a time you felt anger or whatever emotion) even though you may not have experienced the same thing.
Consider other ways (e.g., other paths or strategies in video games, other strategies in sports and board games) you might win the game.	Consider many possibilities for the main character, even if it looks like that person is "stuck."
Be willing to start over in video games; be patient with each piece of a large puzzle; allow yourself to pause a game's session and continue the next day (e.g., chess, puzzles, video games).	Be patient as you wait to discover the outcome or continue to accumulate information; read to understand, not to finish quickly.

She makes notes about what she has learned about their thinking and talking abilities. It becomes apparent to her that the allotted time for talking can easily be wasted if she doesn't teach them what to do.

When she analyzes her observations, Abby decides that she needs to prepare conversational instructions along several lines. She knows that it is important to tap into what students already can do to teach them more ways to talk about books. Keeping the idea of learning by using gaming skills in mind, she designs the lessons in Table 3–1.

Looking back at the list of gaming skills, Abby knows it is reasonable to expect certain skills from students. She also decides to relate the academic skills to specific games she knows her son plays as a way to show students that they already know how to do this thinking in another medium. Even for students who do not play video games, Abby is sure there are sports or board games to which she can connect needed skills.

In general, teachers begin the conversation work by creating partnerships to talk about the content of a read-aloud or shared text. This can also be done with content-area material. Teachers must assess what their students do, as Abby did, in order to make decisions about how to proceed. For example, I could see a class that has little experience talking about books spending more time on this before proceeding. After teaching them to talk with partners about texts, the next step is to let them assign topics to each other.

Chapter 4 takes an in-depth look at how teachers did this with their students for language arts and content-area work. Partner conversations about self-selected topics are important because they teach students to make their brains work to relate to something about which they may know very little—the trunk in grandmother's attic, for example. They must become accustomed to thinking about others' ideas. Students can work in partnerships or groups of three. Teachers should listen in to the conversation work to scaffold student talk and to make assessments for future instruction.

Summary

Early work in writing to prompts centers on being able to engage with an idea and to talk about it for an extended period of time. Taking the time to teach students how to converse is instructional time well spent. Students also benefit from learning to take on others' ideas about texts and from learning ways to figure out what to say when answers are not readily apparent or information seems difficult to recall. This conversation work must be scaffolded by the teacher so that students become adept at talking with partners and in small groups.

To Do in Classrooms

- ❀ Create an atmosphere that encourages conversation and respectful exchanging of ideas

- ❀ Teach students conversation moves (i.e., modes of social and academic discourse)

- Provide time for students to practice talking about shared experiences—read-alouds or other participatory events (e.g., author visits, theater performances, class trips, current events discussions)

- Listen in to students' conversations to assess and scaffold

- Make a class chart, with student input, of successful ways to keep a conversation going and another chart of ways thinkers "grow" new ideas while talking

- Name powerful conversational moves you hear students make, along with students' names

- Assess students' conversational abilities and plan instruction that will lead to talking about literary and academic topics

4

Intellectual Play

Digging into Others' Ideas

It is early October in a fourth-grade class and the teacher, Beth Dropick, is reading aloud *Journey* by Patricia MacLachlan. Her students sit in a circle on beanbags, benches, or the rug as she reads. At times, Beth pauses and asks them to stop and talk with a partner, or to think, or to write in their notebooks (Langer, 1995; Calkins, 2001). She teaches her students to be engaged with the read-aloud because she believes that reading aloud to students offers enormous possibilities for instruction in reading strategies. When the students talk for two minutes to their partners, Beth and I listen to what they say. We are both encouraged and concerned.

Some of their comments demonstrate a grasp of the story and the underlying themes that run through it. For example, two students talk about how Journey must learn to love his grandparents because they are his only family now; they begin a discussion of what a family is. One partnership talks about the symbolism of the photos in the book. A small number of students, however, seem to have little to say beyond, "I don't know. What do you think?" Beth and I exchange glances. Although we know it is important to assess the situation carefully based on other data about these students, we recognize the following work that must be done, particularly because we plan to work on writing to prompts about literature.

⊛ Help them interact insightfully with literature, especially when the difficulty of reading the print is eliminated through read-alouds

- Teach students that talking can help them "invent" something to say about any text

- Teach them that they can take on other students' ideas to talk about

As Beth and I think about each of these points, we realize that all three can help students write to prompts.

When meeting later, Beth and I agree that the students are capable of doing what we've asked because Beth has heard them talk at length about playing baseball and video games. With this in mind, we create a plan for small-group instruction in which we intend to teach students to take on an idea and talk about it as if they were playing video or other games. As students tell us about their processes for playing games, we realize how much they already know. For example, players might begin by assessing the game and deciding what is required to win, they explore menu options for insights into how the game is structured, or they jump into the game and revise as they go along. All these skills could be applied to prompt writing.

This chapter talks about transferring the thinking workshop from gaming to the work in English language arts classes to prepare students for assigned topics about literature. The sections cover one teacher's process of investigating assigned topics with her class, talking with partners about self-selected assigned topics from notebooks, partner-assigned writing in writers' notebooks, and assigning topics in literature class.

The Process of Investigating Assigned Topics

Mary Ellyn Lehner teaches English language arts to sixth graders in middle school. Like me, she is intrigued by the idea of writing to prompts, especially since she worries about the writing mastery tests her students must take. Mary Ellyn runs effective reading and writing workshops. She also must teach one core novel mandated by her district, which she uses as a "mentor" text for reading and writing; that is, she uses it to demonstrate reading and writing strategies and returns to the book all year long for minilessons (Ray, 1999; Calkins, 2001; Angelillo, 2005). Mary Ellyn decides to study students' thinking when they write about their own topics, and whether they can be taught to transfer this same thinking to write well about assigned topics.

While she launches her writing workshop, Mary Ellyn assigns the following prompt to students as a baseline for their prompt writing. She purposely makes the topic bland and broad to see how they will respond.

"Write about your favorite season. It could be a time of year, holiday, sports season, or any other season. Make sure to include why this season is your favorite."

She observes as they write and then collects the writing they did (see Fig. 4–1) to assess what they need.

Mary Ellyn notices that the students' writing is proficient, but when she and I examine it, we agree it lacks voice. There is little elaboration or sentence variation. Some of it sounds stilted, as if the students know they are writing just to fulfill an assignment. In general, we realize her students must learn to write better than this.

At the same time, Mary Ellyn and I teach the students to keep writers' notebooks (Fletcher, 1996). Notebooks are a vehicle for teaching them all the richness of writing and of the thinking behind it. Writers write from the events and experiences of their lives, much of which becomes stories, essays, or poems later on. Using her own notebook, Mary Ellyn demonstrates how she does this. She knows that writers often talk with partners about their writing, but she decides to ask students to write without first talking about their ideas (Fig. 4–2); she hopes to gather information about the value of conversation work before writing.

By studying and comparing the assigned-topic writing and the notebook writing, Mary Ellyn and I notice that in the self-selected topics of the writers' notebooks, students show some internal thinking, extension of ideas, thoughtful selection of nouns and verbs, sensory details, and voice. However, when writing to an assigned topic (Fig. 4–1), they show far less writing skill. Although they attempt to write in complete sentences, their writing is stilted and simplistic. They appear to need instruction in elaboration, internal thinking, specific use of nouns and verbs, making meaning, varying sentence structure, use of dialogue and description, voice, and stamina. Mary Ellyn asks me to help her work within the structure of her writing workshop to strengthen her students' ability to answer prompts, so we decide to do the following.

⊛ Work on extending ideas through conversation and internal dialogue

⊛ Work on strategies for elaboration, including the use of conventions to add details and appositives

William

    My favorite season is Winter.
There are many reasons I like Winter,
but there are three main ones. Those are,
Wrestling starts, Snow, and Christmass.
    First I'll tell you what's so great
about Wrestling. It is very fun, so fun
that it is my favorite sport. There is
no better feeling in the world then
knowing when you get off the mat after
the match is over that you gave it your
all. To me thats winning, no matter
what the score is.

Kevin Galvin   September 8

    My favorite season is fall. This is because of the
sports, activities to do, and all the holidays and party's
Fall is the best season, not to hot, not to cold, and tons
of things to do.
    First is sports. There are lots of exciting sports
to play and watch in the fall. First is baseball. I
play baseball in the fall. It is called fall-ball. Some
games are really cold and windy, but other game are on
beautiful autumn days. Also in the the fall is the World
Series, which is really exciting. A little later in the
season is football. I like the New York Jets. My
brother and I also play in the backyard with dad.
That is fun to. After, we finish playing outside
we go in to watch the Jets or Giants. Sometimes
Mom makes wings. Later on in fall basketball starts.
That is a fun sport to. I play intown and travel.

FIG. 4–1 *Sample of students' writing to a prompt*

William
Myowntopic

"Wham!" My brothers fist collided with my face. Blood was pouring out of my lip. I didn't know I was bleeding untill a salty taste met my tounge. Attracted by the scream I had issued my dad came upstairs. His eyes widening as he saw me, he told me I would need to get stiches As his words hung in the air, I felt as if my death sentence had been prnouced I was very frightend, for I didn't like the idea of a razor sharp needle getting stuk into my skin repetetivly. Now however I won't be afraid of getting stiches ever again. After giving me a small shot the doctor began the stitches. I couldn't even feel the needle go into me! All I felt was a tugging at my lip. When I told the doctor this he just smiled and said, that's beacause I just stuck a needle through you!

FIG. 4–2 *Students' writing in writers' notebooks without prior conversation work*

William
Zoom in

The velvet of its body was soft and worn. The light blue, sewn eyes of what was my favorite stuffed animal when I wasyounger stared at me full of comfort, and understanding There are two ears flopping over the back of his head, their insides insted of the the usuall pink, are green, as are the bottom of his feet. The ever smiling face of Bunny has brightened me up many days in my younger years. He has a long lacy collor going around half his neck, and two silky ribbons pretruble from the middle of it. I always feel calm while I am around Bunny, whenever I was sad he would make me feal better. Though his body was once all together, but it is now seperate from being hugged so many times

Kevin
Free Choice

River

    We were hiking through the woods with our neighbors on a cold October day. It was our first time a this hiking place. My mom said there was a river here. Our neighbors and I were all excited because we wanted to see river badly. We started walking through the trail. A little while later I heard water rushing. I knew it was the river. We started to run to get to it, but when we got there it was just a little ~~stream~~ that was coming from the river. We kept walking. When the trail started circling we realized that we had just done a big circle around the river On the way back my mom said we would get an open view of the river. We heard the sound again It started getting louder. We started running, faster, and faster. Finially the woods stopped and the river was right in front of us. We leaned over the edge and looked at the river. It was beautiful. We were where the river was calm, so in the summer you could swim in' it. There were fish and frogs. I tried to reach over with my net to catch a fish and I fell in. The river was freezing. I climbed out of the river. I was so cold. My mom got me a blanket. And that is my river story.

FIG. 4-2 Continued

Kevin G.   Zooming Oct.
                   In   7

Jets Bear

    Its head is round and puffy like a blown up balloon. The white stitches covering its body. Its dark black eyes starting in the same direction all the time. The beady nose sticking out of its head. There is a small little round mouth surrounded by the pure white fur. As you look farther down the body you see a Jets symbol surrounded by the deep green football. On its right leg their is a NYJ sign for New York Jets. It is green with a little white on its border. On the bears back is the word Jets in a normal font and color. The bear feels soft and is filled with beads inside. If one stitch comes apart the beads will come flying out and the bears loving fur will becomed ripped. The ears are just sticking out of his head like they weren't spoced to be there. This is the Jets bear.

- Work on varying sentence structures through the use of mentor sentences

- Work on stamina for writing longer by teaching them to talk longer

Talking About Self-Selected Assigned Topics From Notebooks

I visit Mary Ellyn's class on a day when she demonstrates exploring an idea in one's notebook through writing. When the students write, Mary Ellyn notices that much of it is exploratory—writing that has little organization but shows that the writer is figuring out what he or she wants to say. She decides that this "figuring out what to say" might have value if it was part of thinking and conversation before writing to prompts.

For the next lesson we plan, I follow up by modeling for the class that writing to a prompt involves valuing one's own thinking and the evolution of an idea. The "responder" must get "inside the prompter's mind" to figure out what the prompter wants—the same way a gamer gets inside the thinking of a game. We ask students to talk in partnerships about this idea of valuing and expanding their thinking while trying to figure out what is required from a prompt.

The following is what some partners had to say.

KAITLIN AND KATY: "Talking helps us figure out the meaning of the prompt as well as the content of what to put in our answers."

JACKIE AND KELLA: "We're trying to figure out easy ways to say the prompt to make it more real to ourselves and our experiences."

ANDREW AND NICK: "First you have to know your enemy, then you have to think of different and similar situations. Just remember to make a list because that's important."

WILLIAM: "Well, you can't give equal importance of each part. You have to decide which part of the prompt is most important and focus on that."

Mary Ellyn and I agree that students seem to understand that talking about the prompt is valuable. We are pleased that they can process their talk metacognitively. The challenge will be to help them use their strategies independently while writing to prompts.

Students Assign Each Other Topics

The next time I meet with Mary Ellyn and her students, they have twelve to fifteen entries in their writers' notebooks. We ask them to look through the notebooks and choose an entry that is very unique to their experience. We want them to challenge each other by assigning that topic to their partners: students therefore are assigning each other topics as practice for thinking about someone else's idea.

Mary Ellyn and I model this when she assigns me her topic—"Running is the most important thing in my life." Of course, I roll my eyes, because I am, ahem, not athletic. But I make use of what I know about friends' running habits, clothing, and diets to talk for a few minutes about something that I know very little about. I take on others' habits as my own and I talk about running as if I actually do it. Alternatively, though running may not be my life, knitting is. So I can think about my passion for knitting as a way to try to write about a passion for running. We begin a chart of ways I push myself to talk about the topic. After that I assign Mary Ellyn a topic from my notebook—"Keeping an herb garden through the winter." This time Mary Ellyn rolls her eyes and everyone laughs, but she draws on gardens she has observed while running in order to talk for a few minutes. Her strategy is added to a list like the following.

How to Talk About Something Unfamiliar

❧ Think of friends who have had the same or similar experiences; try to recall as much detail as possible

❧ Think of times you have been close to the topic or seen it from a distance

❧ Think of ways the topic might fit you before dismissing it

Now it is time for students to skim their notebooks and choose topics to assign to partners; then they are ready to talk. I listen to the following conversations of several partnerships, as does Mary Ellyn.

Nick gives William his topic—"traditions in my family." William says his family doesn't have many traditions, but he uses his own life to imagine what it would be like and offers a substitution by talking about traditions he wishes they had as if they were true.

William gives Nick his topic—"getting stitches." Nick has had stitches so he is able to talk about it. But he says that if he never had had them, he would tell the story of his friend getting stitches as if it were his own. He would draw on his bank of memories.

Jan gives Katy her topic—"I have a cat." Katy doesn't have a cat, so she is ready to think of all the ways the topic doesn't fit her. Then she thinks about the past and decides to tell something unusual that happened to a cat on TV. She connects it to "that's just what cats do when left alone." She adds some description from a photo of a cat on the class calendar and tries to push herself to imagine why "her cat" would be important to her.

Connor gives Jimmy his topic—"What would it be like to be without video games?" Jimmy talks about what it might be like to be in others' shoes and how he would think of activities to fill in the time he spends with games. He also lists things he would do to save money to buy them, and imagines making appointments to play friends' games.

Paul gives Kevin his topic—"cats." Kevin talks about his aunt's cat and says if he didn't know anyone with a cat, he would talk about what they look like and what they do because he's known cats from cartoons, books, and movies.

When we meet again to process their conversation, the students are ready to add some of their ideas to a list like the following.

Students' List of How to Talk About Something Unfamiliar

- I put in a family character so it seems like it happened in my family. —Eric

- I elaborate from an experience I remember from the past. —Gaton

- I find stuff that needs explaining. —Matt

- I look at some parts under my mind's microscope. —Thomas

- I remember a moment like that one. —Chelsea

- I reach down into my mind and remember my emotions. —William

- I look at it from another direction. —Katy

- I think what the author (of the prompt) is like and what she might like to hear. —Jackie

- I think of everything I can about the topic and make a mental list, then I put the picture together. —Eric

Mary Ellyn and I are fascinated by her students' metacognition. She decides to continue this talk by asking students to assign topics and talk about them several times a week. She wants students to have practice taking on an unfamiliar topic and finding strategies to force themselves to keep talking. We both emphasize to students that they are not being encouraged to lie! We just want them to do the intellectual work of owning another's idea, even if they know very little about the subject.

Partner-Assigned Writing in Writers' Notebooks

Kevin and William work together as a partnership. Kevin assigns William the topic of jet skiing, and William assigns Kevin the topic of snapping turtles. Both students talk to each other for five to ten minutes. They are allowed to coach by pointing to the preceding How to Talk . . . list of strategies but not by supplying answers or details. After a short conversation, the students write (see Fig. 4–3).

Mary Ellyn asks the boys, "What thinking did you do in your mind to write about this idea as if it were your own idea?" William says that when he started to think about jet skiing, he remembered that last summer his friend went tubing and told him all about it. So he tried to think about that conversation and relate it to jet skiing: "It set up a chain in my head and that helped me write about it." Kevin agrees: "I had to think about everything I know about the topic and I had to picture it in my head." (They produced the lists shown in Fig. 4–4.)

Mary Ellyn and I pull the class together to review what they are discovering. We know that writing about each other's topics is only the beginning but that, as the ELA teacher, Mary Ellyn must push them to write about literature in the same way. First, we create a new list, as shown in the sidebar.

By this time, the class is beginning to understand and enjoy the inquiry. They like getting increasingly challenging topics from their partners, talking about the topics, writing, and then getting their partners' immediate feedback. Thinking back to the discussion of video games in Chapter 2, you can see that these are some of the same elements of popular games—increasingly challenging, interacting with other gamers, playing, and getting immediate feedback. In the case of writing, the partners are able to

Rehearsal for Writing: Ways to Think About Someone Else's Idea

- Recall all you may know about the idea
- Connect to the idea by thinking about similar experiences you may have had
- Think about the idea as if you are an expert
- Use your imagination to put yourself in someone else's mind and body
- Pretend that you are the person experiencing the idea
- Try to create a picture in your mind by thinking about possible settings, experiences, or any background knowledge you may have about the idea

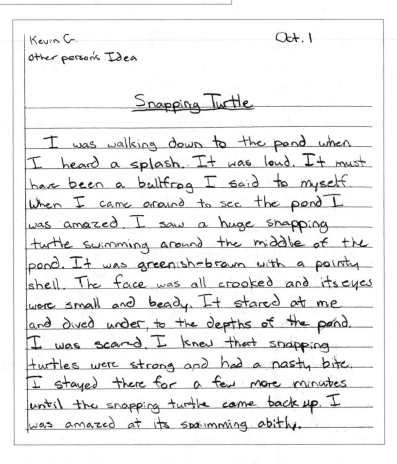

William
Someone else's idea
1st attempt

I've always liked jet skiing. Instead of hitting the slopes, like skiing, you hit the waves. It is hard to keep your body balanced ontop of the water. If you lean too much to one side then "splash!" you literaly hit the waves! Jet skiing is a great way to cool off on a hot day. Could you think of anything more perfect then gliding across crystal clear waters with the spray cooling you of like a nice mist?

Kevin G.   Oct. 1
other person's Idea

Snapping Turtle

I was walking down to the pond when I heard a splash. It was loud. It must have been a bullfrog I said to myself. When I came around to see the pond I was amazed. I saw a huge snapping turtle swimming around the middle of the pond. It was greenish-brown with a pointy shell. The face was all crooked and its eyes were small and beady. It stared at me and dived under, to the depths of the pond. I was scared. I knew that snapping turtles were strong and had a nasty bite. I stayed there for a few more minutes until the snapping turtle came back up. I was amazed at its swimming abithy.

FIG. 4–3 *Two students' first attempt at writing about someone else's ideas*

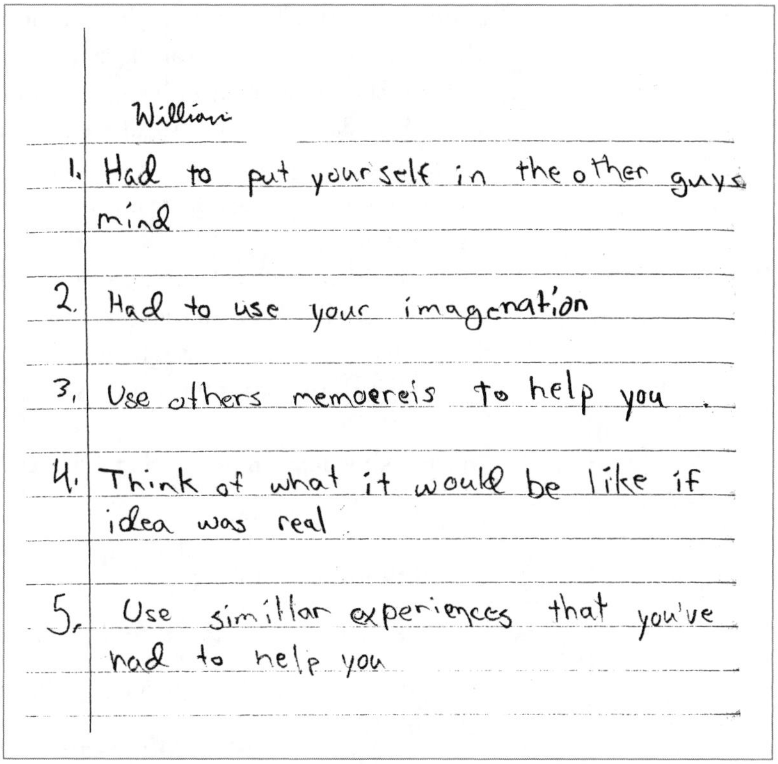

William

1. Had to put yourself in the other guys mind

2. Had to use your imagenation

3. Use others memoereis to help you.

4. Think of what it would be like if idea was real.

5. Use simillar experiences that you've had to help you

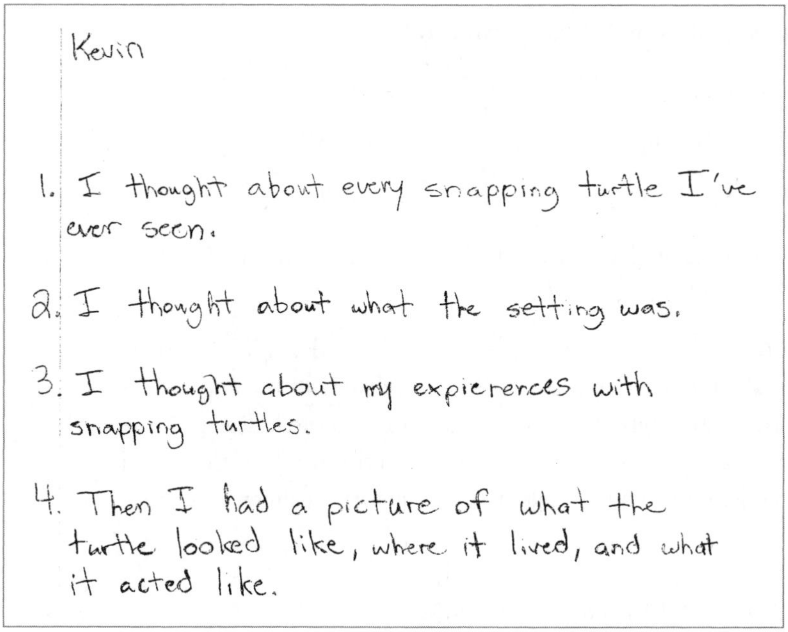

Kevin

1. I thought about every snapping turtle I've ever seen.

2. I thought about what the setting was.

3. I thought about my expierences with snapping turtles.

4. Then I had a picture of what the turtle looked like, where it lived, and what it acted like.

FIG. 4–4 *Two students process their thinking after writing to prompts*

give each other feedback because they are the prompts' creators; they know what they expect to see and can explain that to their partners.

Mary Ellyn continues to work on this with her class for several more weeks. She allots time for assigning topics in partnerships, quality talk, writing, and talking again. On the occasions when students omit prior conversations, she notices that there is a significant difference in the quality of their writing.

By examining William's writing about getting a fish hook caught in his leg before (see Fig. 4–5a) and after (see Fig. 4–5b) meaningful talk, we see the difference in the writing. The following lists show how Mary Ellyn evaluated both versions of this student's writing to a prompt.

Teacher's Evaluation of Writing Prior to Talk

◈ Includes some description

◈ A little internal thinking

◈ Writes about similar experience—fishing with Grandpa

◈ Writes what he knows about fishing—reeling in line, fish fighting

◈ Minimally addresses assigned topic—fish hook piercing leg

Teacher's Evaluation of Writing After Talk

◈ Begins to imagine a possible setting

◈ Begins to pretend that he is experiencing this injury

◈ Recalls what he knows about an injury—pain, swollen leg

◈ Lacks writing stamina as he cleverly dismisses the assigned topic—"I couldn't remember much more."

Mary Ellyn and I meet to process the work we've done. We conclude that talking about unfamiliar topics is helpful for students because it gives them opportunities to rehearse writing and to expand their ideas with the coaching of a partner. The next step is to extend this work to talking and writing about literature and to the practice for answering literary prompts.

Assigning Topics in Literature Class

While Mary Ellyn launches her writing workshop and introduces the intellectual play of writing about someone else's topic, she also launches her

> William
> 10/13
> Write about someone elses idea
>
> "Whoa, thats a big 'un!" On the end of
> my line was a huge bass, must of been at
> least 3 feet long, and about 50 pounds.
> And it was fighting like mad! Let
> me explain a little. My grandpa and
> I were on a fishing trip together in our
> favorite spot, A place we call "Fish
> Haven" because it is swarming with bass
> and flounder." Anyways I didn't think _and it was a trip I will never forget_
> that first bite of the day would
> fight so hard, It took all my
> strenghth just to real in a few inches
> of line, But what a beauty it was.
> Pale pink like the new full moon,
> with glittering stripes. When I finally
> got on land it still wasn't coming
> quitly, so when I got it of the hook
> the line snapped back the hook went
> into my leg, It was agony beond
> anything I ever expeirienced (and I've
> experienced alot of pain), Even worse
> the barbed wire prevented it from
> coming out!

FIG. 4–5a *Student's writing prior to talk that teacher processed*

reading workshop (Calkins, 2001). In her district, she is required to have each class read one core novel per year; in sixth grade it is *Number the Stars* by Lois Lowry. She makes a wise decision to use the book as a mentor text in writing workshop to study Lowry's writing for style and writing strategies, as well as in reading workshop to teach strategies good readers use to access meaning in any text.

Mary Ellyn wants her students to understand that their study of this book will serve as a community-building experience, and that they will refer to the text all year. She is not interested in *teaching the book*. She

William
After talk

    I woke up in a room I didn't know. White drapes hung around the window, and a red cross was above the door. Wait a second a red cross! I was in the hospital, but why? A glint of silver caught my eye. I shifted around in my bed to see better and winced slightly at a pain in my leg. It was a gleaming fishing hook. Now I remembered! I was casting my fishing line when my dog, spot, ran in front of me, so I jerked my line back. The next thing I knew, I was in excrutiating pain. My line was behind me, and when I tried to real it in the pain in my leg swelled almost past endurance. That's when I relized that the hook was in my leg. I couldn't remember much more, all I knew was that the barb made it very painful to take out the hook.
    I pulled my leg out from under my bed sheet, there were a couple of stitches along a curved line. Now all that remains is a thin scar, my only reminder of what a fishing hook feels like.

FIG. 4–5b *Student's writing after talk that teacher processed*

matches her students to independent books they can read at their individual levels (Atwell, 1998; Calkins, 2001; Fountas and Pinnell, 2001; Krashen, 2004; Lesesne, 2003) and expects them to apply the strategies she teaches from *Number the Stars* to their own reading.

By the end of October, Mary Ellyn expects the work of talking and writing about each other's topics to help students write about literature. Her students keep a readers' notebook, where they record ideas and evidence from texts, as well as list the books they've read and notes about Mary Ellyn's minilessons on reading strategies. In general, the notebooks are open-ended. Mary Ellyn has taught them some ways to think about texts (Angelillo, 2003a; Probst, 2004), and she looks to see that they are using these strategies to drive their reading and reading responses.

Reading literature and writing about it is more than just getting the plot, setting, and characters. Throughout time, authors have struggled with many of the same ideas, and struggled to understand the human condition. All the instruction on elements of story and literary devices is useless if it does not point students toward exploring some universal themes humanity continues to try to understand. Of course, students also benefit from learning that reading books can be pleasurable and entertaining (much the same as gaming is!) and that reading can influence a person's personality and behavior (Rosenblatt, 1995). In *Literature as Exploration*, Rosenblatt notes the following.

> [The child who reads] learns to imaginatively "put himself into the place of the other fellow." He [sic] becomes better able to foresee the possible repercussions of his own actions in the life of others. In his daily relations with other people, such sensitivity is precious. Through literature the individual may develop the habit of sensing the subtle transactions of temperament on temperament; he may come to understand the needs and aspirations of others; and he may thus make more successful adjustments in his daily relations with them. . . . A democratic society, whose institutions and political and economic procedures are constantly being developed and remolded, needs citizens with the imagination to see what political doctrines mean for human beings.
>
> It has been said that if our imaginations functioned actively, nowhere in the world would there be children who were starving. (1995, 176)

Like so many teachers, Mary Ellyn recognizes the responsibility of teaching students to respond to literature. While she expects her students will remain active engagers with their books, she decides to see what benefit talk about a literature prompt has on student writing. She chooses a quote from *Number the Stars*. Then she organizes the class into "talk groups" in which they have the opportunity to both figure out what the quote means and to negotiate what they would write about it. Both she and I listen to their conversations; part of one is shown here.

Edited Transcript of a Talk Group Excerpt of Conversation

WILLIAM: She wouldn't have named the book that if there wasn't some good reason.

GATON: I think that the stars means the stars of David that they all wear.

WILLIAM: It can't just be about their religion. *(goes to look through text)* Wait, I think I found something that supports your idea, Gaton.

MATT: Maybe it's that there are as many stars of David as there are stars in the sky.

GATON: So you're saying that the star of David connects with stars of different kinds.

MATT: Not movie stars. *(all laugh)*

DAVE: So I think we could take Gaton's idea and write about saving the Jews. We could find examples from the text to support that. You know, examples that prove that what Lois Lowry wants to say.

WILLIAM: What did we think she was saying?

DAVE: That the Jews are like the stars in the sky and you can't count them all.

WILLIAM: No, I think she's saying that we can't count them all, but God can, so he knows every Jew and every person and cares about them all.

MATT: Yeah. Write that down!

WILLIAM: We have a few good ideas, so we all have to decide which one we want to write about. But we don't all have to write about the same thing.

After fifteen minutes of talk, Mary Ellyn calls students back together. She gives them a few minutes to record notes (Fig. 4–6) of their conversations. Then she asks them to talk again for two minutes to confirm and clarify their thoughts. Once they have done this, she gives them fifteen minutes to write their responses. As students write, Mary Ellyn and I make the following three important observations.

❋ Students who didn't have rich conversations (merely repeated the quote, didn't connect quote to the book) didn't write more than a few sentences

❋ Some students copied the quote onto their papers—this must indicate some previous habits or the need to see the quote in front of them, or it was a delaying tactic

❋ Some students use their notes and their conversations to write thoughtful responses

Think about bravery and courage. Does bravery mean being unafraid, or does it mean doing something daring even if you are afraid? What examples of courage and bravery can you find in this text? Explain.

Relate Number the Stars to your own life experiences. Who do you know that's brave? What did she or he do? With your group, make a list of qualities that might show a person's courage. Connect your ideas about bravery to characters in this text.

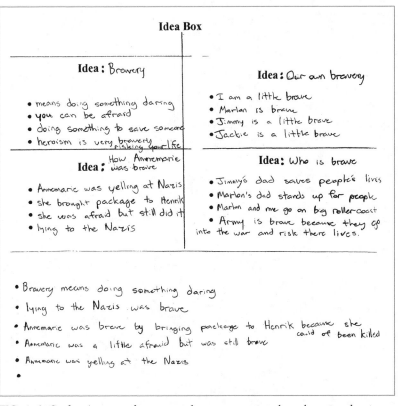

Idea Box

Idea: Bravery

- means doing something daring
- you can be afraid
- doing something to save someone
- heroism is very bravery risking your life

Idea: Our own bravery

- I am a little brave
- Marlon is brave
- Jimmy is a little brave
- Jackie is a little brave

Idea: How Annemarie was brave

- Annemarie was yelling at Nazis
- she brought package to Henrik
- she was afraid but still did it
- lying to the Nazis

Idea: Who is brave

- Jimmy's dad saves people's lives
- Marlon's dad stands up for people
- Marlon and me go on big roller-coast
- Army is brave because they go into the war and risk there lives.

- Bravery means doing something daring
- lying to the Nazis was brave
- Annemarie was brave by bringing package to Henrik because she could of been killed
- Annemarie was a little afraid but was still brave
- Annemarie was yelling at the Nazis
-

FIG. 4–6 *Students' notes and responses after a conversation about the assigned topic*

From what my group and I talked about I figured out what the meaning of bravery is. Bravery is doing something you don't want to do. There are a lot of people in the world who are brave. For an example, someone who is brave in the text <u>Number The Stars</u> is Annemarie. Annemarie is brave because she risked her life for her uncle Henrik. She went out on a cold and damp October morning to deliver this package. Annemarie could have gotten caught by the German soldiers. This is why Annemarie was brave. Another person who was brave was Uncle Henrik. Uncle Henrik was brave because he was the one who took the Jews across to Sweeden. If a soldier found the Jews that were hideing under the boat, Uncle Henrik would have died. He risked his life for Jewish people. Another example of a brave person is Peter. Peter was brave because he was a Resistance fighter. He helped the Jews and other people survive. He is the one who was a part of the tissue making. He

made a tissue so that the dogs could not sniff out the people. This saved a lot of Jews! This is why Peter was brave. Last but not least another person who was brave was Mama. She was brave because she took the risk of leaving her two girls alone when the soldiers could have found them. Mama went out with the Rosens to make sure they were safe. These are some examples of bravery from the text <u>Number The Stars</u>.

FIG. 4–6 *Continued*

November 3
L.A. 02 / Rdg. 03

    Annemarie was brave in the book, Number the Stars. Annemarie was brave by bringing the package to Uncle Henrik. Without the drug that was in that package, the Jews in the bottom of the boat most likely would have been found. Even though Annemarie was scared she did the task because she was brave. She was also brave by yelling and lying to the Nazis. If she didn't lie to them about what she was doing they would of found out about the whole plan. She was also brave by yelling. She knew she had to do something and she did it. When Uncle Henrik said," it is easier to be brave if you don't know everything," it helped Annemarie later on in the book when she took the package to Uncle Henrik. She didn't know why Uncle Henrik needed it or what it was but that helped her become more brave. If she knew what was in it she might have been more nervous and slipped up or not been able to stand up to the Nazis. This is the act of heroism that Annemarie did to save a lot of Jews.

FIG. 4–6 Continued

When the two of us talk with the students the next day, we compliment them for the confidence many of them show in their writing. One student, Zack, says that he doesn't like to read books that are confusing, but when he talks with his group, much of his confusion is cleared up. He's able to write better because of the conversations. Nate also tells us that, for the first time in a reading response, he felt like he was writing for himself rather than for the teacher; several others agree: The talk groups helped them own the topic and shift their perspective to writing for themselves to explore an idea.

Together with the students, Mary Ellyn and I conclude that whenever possible, it is beneficial to talk in small groups about an assigned topic, then to write notes for a few minutes before writing responses. The challenge is to practice this helpful talk long enough so that students can learn to have an internal dialogue on occasions when they cannot talk about their ideas in a group.

Summary

In reading and writing workshops, students know they can value their thinking and honor each other's thoughts. Teachers can teach them to begin the work of thinking about others' topics by allowing them to assign topics to each other in partnerships and to talk about them. Once students have had practice talking and getting feedback from each other about assigned topics, teachers can have them practice with assigned topics from a read-aloud or shared text. It is critical to note that this work does not take the place of the independent reading and writing in workshops, but is meant to support it in order to prepare for times when students must think and write to prompts. As always, ongoing assessment of student work is key to planning additional instruction.

To Do in Classrooms

* Establish solid writers' notebooks and a class read-aloud

* Teach students to value their thinking by talking about notebook writing

* Ask student to choose one topic from their notebooks and assign it to a partner to think about

- Process the type of thinking required to effectively think about someone else's idea, especially when unfamiliar with the topic

- Ask student to take notes and then write about the topics after talking

- Scaffold the work into reading workshop by assigning a topic from the class read-aloud

- Provide time to talk in small groups, to take notes, and to write

- Assess to determine what to teach next

5

The Daily Work
Using Prompts to Lift the Level of Student Work

The work Mary Ellyn Lehner and I did in her classroom (see Chapter 4) made me think about the brain work of prompts and how students are taught to engage with assigned topics in school. How are students taught to think about prompts, as opposed to being given formulas to follow while writing? I took this question with me everywhere I went, and asked as many young people as I could. I asked my young nieces and the neighbors' children. I asked students at weekend religious schools and kids at the gym. I asked college students and graduate students:

What do you do when you have to think about someone else's idea?
What is your process for answering a prompted question?

While visiting some friends in Boston, I had dinner one night with their daughter, Adina, and her friend Katy, both in middle school. These two young women were articulate and thoughtful, and their comments aligned with much of my own research. They said they dislike writing about literature in their English classes because writing prompts are often shallow and narrow, as if teachers are merely checking to see if they've read the book. However, both girls said they like the exercise of debating and arguing about texts, and consider it similar to playing a basketball game, for which you have to move around to get anywhere. In effect, they said they like playing with ideas, but not teachers' ideas!

In their independent reading, the girls were sharing *Dangerous Angels* by Francesca Lia Block, and said they had lots to talk about from the book. I asked them, "Suppose I *told* you what to talk or write about in this book?" Both girls frowned.

"It would have to be something that would make us think in order for it to be worthwhile," Katy said. "Otherwise it's a waste of time."

Adina nodded and said. "Yeah, it's got to add to the experience and pleasure of the book, not test me on literary elements or themes."

"Tell me what you mean by 'add to the experience,'" I said.

"It's got to make me think about how to use my life experiences and literary elements to figure out new ideas," Adina responded.

"I think it's a good idea for a teacher to point students in a direction for discussion, but not to test us on the book. That sets a low standard. Kids figure out pretty fast that some teachers don't think they're smart enough to talk about ideas," Katy added.

"Or the fact that in order to talk about a book, you have to have read it!" Adina said.

All the way home on the train, I thought about what Adina and Katy had said and how smart their thinking was. It echoed much of what I hear almost every time I talk to young people about writing to prompts. While they do not like to write about books in English class, they do like book discussions (Reeves, 2003). However, when writing is required, they expect to be challenged, not tested. They do not object to writing prompts as long as the prompts are intelligent, appropriate, and allow them to think. These comments, from Adina, Katy, and from scores of other students, make me think about implications for using prompts to lift the level of students' thinking during reading and writing workshops. With this in mind, this chapter examines partner or book club discussions that grow from assigned topics, support for student thinking and writing to assigned topics (e.g., themes, other literary elements), how to use prompts wisely to get the most benefit from author studies, and teaching assigned writing for nonfiction studies.

Discussions That Grow From Assigned Topics

One of the main purposes of partnerships is for students to support each other while reading the same book. Early on, teachers can use this support system for partners to help each other talk and write to literary prompts. In classrooms where students are primarily reading independent books suited to their reading levels, along with read-aloud and shared reading texts, two students on the same or similar levels are paired to read the same text. While some students may just support each other with the print, partnerships serve other functions as well. The partners learn to plan reading together, both in amount and in focus. They learn to incorporate whole-class

There are three structures for instruction in reading and writing workshops. Use of all of them provides for an effective, supportive learning environment for students and allows for differentiated instruction.

- *Whole-class instruction:* Usually conducted through intense, direct teaching that lasts ten to fifteen minutes; such "minilessons" contain instruction in reading or writing strategies that the teacher has determined the entire class needs based on an assessment (Anderson, 2005) and what's in the school or district curriculum. The teacher models or demonstrates what students are expected to learn rather than merely assigning work.

- *Small-group instruction:* The teacher determines the needs of students through assessment and gathers small groups for direct instruction tailored to something specific (Calkins, 2001; Fountas and Pinnell, 2001). These groups are temporary, and the teacher can use them to support high achievers, as well as strugglers. Ongoing assessment is required to make such groups successful.

- *Individual instruction:* This component is the most powerful structure. A teacher meets with individual students to determine each's needs. Then she or he *teaches* a strategy to one student. Recordkeeping, planning, and student accountability are critical to the success of this component (Anderson, 2000; Calkins, Hartman, and White, 2005).

FIG. 5–1 *Organizing instructional frameworks*

instruction (see Fig. 5–1) into partner reading, and they hold each other accountable for reading, thinking, and planning for conversation.

The reading in partnerships leads to taking notes in preparation for, or as a result of, conversations by writing on sticky note tags and/or index cards or by responding in readers' notebooks (see Fig. 5–2). Later in the year, partnerships can join together into book clubs in which three to five students choose and read a book together (Daniels, 2001; Calkins, 2001). Although not *all* partner or book club conversations are written down, many should be. Students need to use their conversations to grow new ideas and they need to record these ideas as evidence of their work together.

When planning for instruction and considering how to introduce prompts into work, teachers must consider what the prompt is for, whether the teaching matches the purpose of the prompt, and how to support students as they engage with the prompt. A prompt can serve several purposes, including the following.

- Pushing students to see something, such as a literary element, in a new or original way

- Supporting students' interaction with the text by helping them make connections that build understanding

- Challenging students to consider a text in a new way, to draw on previous knowledge, or to think across texts

Most teachers use reading response as a way to determine comprehension. While each type of entry in this menu of possibilities list requires students to understand the text, they must also understand the purpose of each response. The teacher should demonstrate each through her or his own writing so that students learn to use the readers' notebook for the following.

- To collect thoughts and ideas about text

- To record evidence from text in support of an idea

- To record and reflect on facts, especially during research

- To record partnership and book club conversations

- To take notes from a read-aloud

- To take notes in preparation for conversations

- To note new understandings that come from rereading

- To reflect on facts or events and/or changes in a text

- To record connections and build understanding from them

- To collect sticky notes when done with a text

- To reread to build new thinking and then write more

- To use shorter notes as a basis for longer entries

- To freewrite to access thinking and to build understanding

- To make T-charts to record events from the text and reflections on what they might mean

- To make plans for more reading

- To reflect on one's reading process and progress

- To make plans for writing about reading

- To plan and organize genres of writing about reading

- To plan using one text in several genres (e.g., "How can I use all this information I collected on Egypt in another genre, such as editorial or story, after I complete my required feature article?")

- To record texts read throughout the year and to evaluate one's choices and reading progress

- To write about any of the "ways to think about books" from the class chart

- To try out language for longer writing about reading genres

- To record useful quotes from books and reflect on them

- To make connections across books

- To muse about language, authors, ideas, characters, and so on

- To record and reflect on the use of literary devices

- To collect examples of literary devices from texts

- To build ongoing understanding of why writers use literary devices and how readers use them to build comprehension

- To note favorite parts of books and reflect on why they're selected

- To record information from book reviews, author visits, and other literary events

- To rehearse note-taking and writing

- To collect intriguing words

- To reflect on connections across texts and media

- To make charts to support thinking and/or gathering of evidence

- To connect all reading back to a philosophy of literacy and why humans read and/or write

- "To find places within assignments that activate their passions" (Romano, 2004, 7)

FIG. 5–2 *Responding in readers' notebooks*

No matter what, a prompt should do more than merely test whether students have read the book. A brief conversation can reveal that immediately. A prompt must involve thinking about and wrestling with ideas much the way a game does; few successful game players play passively. Prompts should not encourage passivity in learning, thinking, or writing. So, teachers must examine their teaching to be sure students are taught to engage with the ideas in prompts and to be sure their expectations are very clear.

Most often, when students meet in partnerships, teachers give them choices about what to write. This writing could indicate their progress through the book in terms of following "lines of thinking," such as tracing the development of a character or the impact of setting on the plot. In some cases, students use the teacher's minilessons as guides for what to follow in their books and write accordingly because all reading and writing is recursive (Bruner, 1986). Sometimes, students demonstrate remarkable insights in their conversations, and write these in their notebooks.

Other times, teachers find that students do not transfer the important parts of their conversations into their writing. Unfortunately, this leads some teachers to conclude that they must assign topics to students. Assigned topics should always serve a *purpose;* teachers must always keep this in mind. Although it is not the best way to check students' reading, teachers sometimes want them to demonstrate that they are using what is being taught (see Table 5–1). In the case of students who do not write as well as they talk (i.e., transfer their insightful conversations to paper), it is better to work on techniques and strategies for capturing thinking than to assign topics with little purpose.

Strategies to Help Students Capture Conversations on Paper

- Have students audiotape conversations, then listen to them and write down the best parts

- Demonstrate having a conversation with another teacher; stop and model by thinking aloud what you would write down

- Teach students to use key words, sentence fragments, phrases, page numbers, and codes to mark their thinking

- Ask students to listen to each other's conversations in groups and to take notes on them, then offer the notes to the conversers as a gift

- Have students practice stopping a conversation every few minutes to restate what they've said and to decide whether to write anything down

- Ask students to reread notes at the end of conversations to add anything important they've left out

- Teach highlighting to prioritize important points

- Make note-taking a collaborative experience for everyone in a group

- Teach students to hold on to thinking with a symbol or a picture

TABLE 5–1 Some Purposes for Assigning Topics for Readers' Notebooks

Purpose of Assigned Topic	Teaching to Match Purpose
To use and practice current teaching	Write in your notebooks using one of the teaching points from today's or yesterday's lessons. For example, if working on character development, most entries will be about that.
To demonstrate utilization of prior teaching	Show what you know about how writers create full characters to explore the main character in your book.
To dig into a concept with increasing depth	Last month we learned several facts about how writers use setting. Today, I'd like you to write more about how setting helps you understand your book. Push yourself to write about it more fully.
To layer current instruction onto prior instruction	Show how you can put together today's minilesson with one item from the chart of old minilessons. Reflect on how it helps you understand.
To explore a new concept (e.g., intertextuality, self-assessment, literary devices)	Write three entries in which you push yourself to consider today's minilesson as it relates to the book you are reading.
To push together concepts	Connect what you know about [setting] as a way to understand a [character].
To practice the process of engagement	Write about how you wrap your mind around the book you are reading and how what you already know about books helps you do that.

⊛ Create a note-taking rubric to show students the main points you are looking for (Angelillo, 2003a, 135)

Let's imagine a typical classroom where some students follow through diligently and use their notes and readers' notebooks to record their thinking and partnership conversations about a text (Angelillo, 2003a). This work provides students with numerous opportunities to expand on their thinking and to record their conversations. However, as I visit classrooms and read student notebooks, I often notice other trends as well. Some students get stuck in a rut and write the same things over and over ("Today we talked about the main character . . .") without digging deeper or thinking about how their conversation might change based on their progress through the book. Their entries are arbitrary—one day writing about character, the next writing about setting, the next retelling (okay, most often retelling). Students who flit from one kind of response to another do not understand that talking and writing should help them come to new understandings about a text.

The readers' notebook must have *purpose*, and it can only have purpose if students are taught to respond purposefully. Thinking aloud for students is one way to teach them to do this (Ray, 1999; Wilhelm, 2001). More teacher guidance might benefit students, but not by assigning topics every day. Daily assignments carry the message that teachers believe students can't think for themselves, while carefully planned guidance scaffolds student thinking and learning. The type of guidance I propose is working with students to help them understand that certain types of entries align well with certain texts, in addition to challenging them to think and talk about a text in one way (i.e., the assigned topic).

On the other hand, occasional practice with writing to prompts while students are in partnerships or book clubs gives them the opportunity to talk out their answers with peers. Teachers might even play a What If? game with students, giving them an opportunity to play with ideas: "What if Abraham Lincoln were president today? What if Gilly Hopkins' mother came back? What if Beethoven met a hip-hop singer?" The seemingly outrageous conversations that might be sparked by such speculations give students ways to imagine how to respond to them. Thus, one state's writing exam prompt—"What did you find in your grandmother's trunk?"—becomes less foreign to students who have had experience playing with the mulling around of ideas and forcing connections, even when they do not have a lot of information.

Teachers should scaffold the conversations to ensure that students are equipped with some information so that they can knead it into a conversation. Providing them with positive prompt talking and writing experiences helps build their confidence. Therefore, it is important to craft prompts that demonstrate the following.

◈ Writing about the process of engaging with the prompt

◈ Writing toward the prompt as self-assessment of reading

◈ Writing by applying class teaching to the prompt

◈ Original thinking sparked by the prompt

Table 5–2 lists examples of how teachers might think aloud about each of the preceding points.

In each case, the partner or book club discussion supports the notebook writing. Students consider the prompt, talk about it, and then write their

TABLE 5–2 Writing and Thinking Prompts for Teachers to Model

Prompt Writing That Demonstrates Thinking	Teaching Through Modeling
Engaging with the prompt	I make a quick list of what I know about this. If I know very little, then I think of others I know who have had the same experience, or I relate it to my own life. I'm willing to struggle to understand it because I know there is not one answer, and my brain can figure out ways to get hold of it.
Using the prompt as self-assessment	I read the prompt and I think about what it is asking. If I don't understand it, I read it again. If I have a problem wrapping my mind around it, I know I have to practice by batting around ideas with a partner.
Applying class teaching to the prompt	I know that responding to a prompt doesn't exist in a vacuum. I can use all I've learned this year (and refer to charts and my notebook) to figure out what to say. I can choose from all the lessons my teacher has taught all year, and use all that work in reading and writing workshop to help me. Then I make a decision: "Can I use what I know about the writer's craft to help me, or about an author's work, or about elements of the story? What will help me most?"
Original thinking sparked by the prompt	Sometimes I think I am not interested in a prompt, so I have nothing to say. Then I discover that I know something I can use and apply it to the prompt. So, for example, I might use what I know about how difficult it is to learn to knit to think about a prompt about playing baseball, even if I know nothing about baseball. And the prompt on baseball might make me decide to find out something about baseball after all.

responses. Chapter 8 looks at a unit of study on writing to prompts that builds on the talk and notebook writing done here.

Support for Student Thinking and Writing to Assigned Topics

In Erik Perotti's sixth-grade class, students gather in small groups to talk about their read-aloud book, *Tuck Everlasting* by Natalie Babbitt. Erik tells me he wants to scaffold his students' learning to develop strength in finding their own topics for literary essays, so he uses the read-aloud of this book as a way to get them thinking about themes. In reading workshop, Erik and I usually let ideas about themes arise from students' discussions and then ask them to collect evidence. We both recognize, however, that when they enter middle school the following year, they will be required to write to literature prompts much more often. Therefore, we design a careful study to support this skill. This study is not to teach the formula of a five-paragraph essay, which Tom Romano says has "skewed voice, blocked energy, drained juice" (2004, 6). Erik's study is on the intellectual engagement with an idea, not on the formula of the school essay.

After reading aloud about a quarter of Babbitt's book, Erik identifies two possible interpretations of one theme and provides students with many opportunities to talk, take notes, and find evidence in the text. Essentially, he teaches that the same text can be used to support opposing ideas—a major concept in the teaching of critical literacy (McLaughlin and DeVoogd, 2004; Rosenblatt, 1995). Erik gives students lots of time to think about which side of the theme they prefer and to refer to the text. He provides them with copies of the book while in discussion groups, though during the read-aloud, they do not have the text.

The prompt for conversation and writing is: "Using evidence from *Tuck Everlasting*, do you think it is a blessing or a curse to live forever?" This prompt drives students' small-group discussions, their notes, and eventually the essays they write.

Erik gives his students freedom to write about other ideas from the text in their readers' notebooks because he doesn't want them to believe there are only two themes in this or any book. But, by guiding their work through the two-sided prompt, he helps students learn the process of engaging with ideas and using conversation to strengthen their thinking (see sidebar). Erik focuses students' thinking on the prompt's theme in the following three ways.

- How it makes them think about their own lives and the world (opinion)

- How the characters feel about the idea (text evidence)

- How it changes their view of life (literature as life exploration)

Their conversations and notes focus on one idea and lead them to write essays that thoroughly take on one side of the theme and examine it in depth (see Fig. 5–3).

Erik's colleague, fifth-grade teacher Jane Levy, decides to prepare her students for his class the following year. She meets with small groups or partnerships and assigns them a topic to pay attention to while reading, based on minilessons she's already done. For instance, Jane teaches elements of story (e.g., plot, setting, character, movement through time, change) early in the school year, and she asks students to "live off" that teaching—refer back to it—for a long time. When she meets with students, she consults the charts the class made about stories' elements, and she assigns each group an element to follow as they read their partnership or group book.

"Students have to know that everything I teach is important, and have trust that they can and should use it again and again," Jane tells me in our debriefing. "Of course, that means that I must be careful to craft excellent and meaningful minilessons." Jane is a wise teacher. She teaches thoroughly and carefully and then holds her students accountable by looking for evidence of her teaching in all their work from that point on. Since they have studied story elements already, she reinforces these concepts while expecting students to use them to build new understandings about literature. Erik agrees with Jane. When I meet with him, he says:

My students learn that reading and writing are like math. In math class, students know that you don't forget addition when you move on to the next topic. You need addition to help you understand algebra. And you need elements of story or features of nonfiction text to help you understand the next book you are reading. And even more important for prompt writing, all previous learning is a bank from which you can draw knowledge when answering a prompt.

Rather than have students write essays, Jane asks them to write literary letters to her (Atwell, 2002); each one should examine the topic or story element she assigned to each partnership, along with quotes and evidence

Literary Essay
By: Hannah Bernhard

 Living forever and never growing old is a fate worse than death. In Tuck Everlasting, a novel by Natalie Babbitt, The Tucks try to cope and live with their secret, that they'll live forever and never grow old, and never live a normal life like regular people.
 The Tuck family, Mother Mae, Father Tuck, Brothers Miles and Jesse, cannot live a normal life because they are not normal people.

 The Tucks must live their whole life in secrecy. They can't make any friends, for the friends would grow and they wouldn't. They can't let anyone find out about their secret because everybody would want to take a drink from the spring, and that would be the end of each and every life cycle. The Tucks must be so cautious about where they go, and for how long. It's like they're just put earth, nobody even knows that they're alive. "The boys don't come home very often," says Mother Mae to Winnie. What she's really saying is that they *can't* come home very often, for fear that too many people would see them, and hint on to their secret. They can't even stay in the same place for very long, because people would start to see that they never grow any older, and they've looked the same for 87 years.

 It's horrible that the Tucks can't be exposed and make friends with regular people. They constantly have to keep moving. They only have each other in the whole entire world, and they're all together only once every ten years. They're not a real family, for they can never be together for more than a week. Mae always talks about how she can only be with her whole family every ten years. This shows that she can't even see her two sons for years because of the secret of the spring. I think that I would rather die than only be able to see my kids every ten years, and to have to live my whole life as a secret, just because I wouldn't be able to die.

 Throughout the novel the Tucks must live their life knowing that they will never complete the natural life cycle. They can never get any older or die, and since they can never die, they will never fully complete the life cycle like Winnie can. "That's what we Tucks are Winnie. Stuck, so's we can't move on. We ain't part of the wheel. Dropped of Winnie, left behind," exclaims Father Tucks as he is trying to explain the importance of the secret of the spring to Winnie. The Tucks will never life a normal life and will never complete a life cycle because they can't die.

 Imagine knowing that you can never be a normal person, simply because you can't carry out the life cycle. This is what it was like for the Tuck family. They simply can never die. This is a fate much worse than death because you can never carry out the full life cycle. Every normal living thing has to be able to die at one point in its life, and the Tucks can't. They're not normal people anymore. Like Father Tuck said, they're simply stuck.

 Living a life where you can't make friends, you're always moving, and you basically have to keep you existence a secret is definitely a fate worse than death to me.

 The most important point is that there are more cons than pros to be able to live forever. You won't be able to complete a life cycle if you life forever, because you would never be able to die. You would live your whole life in secrecy, because you couldn't take a chance of more people finding out about the secret spring. The book shows how depressed the Tucks are while living forever. If I had to live a life like the Tucks had to, I wouldn't want to live at all, and I think most people would agree.

FIG. 5–3 *Four students with diverse skill levels write about a common theme in* Tuck Everlasting

Tuck Everlasting

I think that living forever is fate worse than death. In the book Tuck Everlasting the Tuck family has a secret like no other they are forced to live with the fact of living forever and never growing old.

Father Tuck in chapter 2 is dreaming and Mae wakes him up and he says "Why did you have to wake me up. I was having that dream again the good one where we were all in heaven and we had never heard of Treegap." This a great example of Father Tuck wishing that he had never drunk from the spring and that he isn't living life to the fullest.

How can you ever really live if you don't die? The reason life is so great is because of the fear of death. If you couldn't die than you would live recklessly and not try to do great things before you died because you would have all the time in the world. That wouldn't be fun if every one was not careful and do not care what happens. The biggest thrills in life come after taking risks. Living forever would take all the risk out of life and with that all of the thrills.

In chapter 12 Father Tuck talks to Winnie about how the tucks are rocks stuck on the side of the road that keeps going and changing and that they just exist. He also says that you can't call it living what we got because you can't have living without dying. It's all one big circle. That's what life is.

The Tucks just exist. They will never be able to live a normal life. Life is like a big mountain. The tucks have been climbing and climbing trying to reach the top. Until they drank from the spring and now they're just stuck unable to climb any higher.

Without fearing death how can you ever really live?

After reading this book I have realized why Winnie did not drink the water from the spring. Her life would be miserable. There would be nothing to look forward to because you could do anything any time you wanted. There would be no excitement in your life. I guess it would be sort of fun at first but after awhile you would be doing the same thing for ever just waiting for something to change but nothing ever would because you would live forever.

Literary Essay
By Josh Leff

Thesus statement

Living forever and never growing old is a fate worse than death.

Transition sentence

In the book Tuck Everlasting by Natile Babit, the Tuck family can never grow old and die.

General Statement

The Tuck family cannot live a normal life.

Support

Tuck once talked to Whinnie about how horrible living forever was. He said you get off the wheel of life "You don't live, you just are there" said Tuck. Life is like a wagon, if you fall off, the wagon will not stop for you, and you can't catch up to it."

Connection

I agree with Father Tuck. Some people have religious beliefs that people should live and then eventually die. I am one of those people. Living forever throws you off the wheel of life and you are unable to follow your religious beliefs.

General Statement

Living forever and never growing old throws you off of the wheel of life.

Important Point

Living forever does not mean happiness. In Tuck Everlasting, the book shows that living forever can mean no friends, and no human contact. That makes life for the Tucks depressing. This book shows that you have one life, but if you don't have a natural life where you follow your own life cycle, you can't say you are actually living.

FIG. 5–3 *Continued*

Literary Essay
Tuck Everlasting

By Jessica Chance

Living forever and never growing old is a fate worse than death. In the novel Tuck Everlasting, by Natalie Babbit there is a family called the Tucks and they have a problem…

The Tuck family is Mother Mae, Father Tuck, and brothers Miles and Jesse. They do not live a normal life at all, they have to live forever.

The Tuck family doesn't live an exciting life, they live a lonely life. Mae and Tuck only see their sons once every ten years. In chapter 2 Mae states "But I can't wait to see them. Anyways it has been ten years since I went to Treegap." Treegap was the closest town around. Mae was so excited to see her boys that she was willing to risk the "eternal" secret that she and her family have. Jesse and Miles never see each other either. They always have to travel so no one notices that they aren't changing. They travel around the country not staying in one place too long. They can't get married, or have any friends so they are always by themselves defending a secret.

I feel really bad for the Tucks. They must have a sad and lonely life. Not having any friends, never even getting to see their family. I would not want to be separated from my mom, dad and sister for ten years at a time. I would be sad and miserable, just like the Tuck family. In chapter 10 Winnie say to Mae "that's too bad," she said glancing shyly at Mae "always moving around and never having any friends or anything."

In this book the Tucks are out of the life cycle. How? Well since they have to live forever, they can never die and dying is part of the cycle. Almost all the Tuck family wants to die. Miles and Tuck are firm about it. In chapter 2 Tuck states "I was having that dream again, the **good one,** where we are all in heaven and never heard of Treegap." Tuck wants to die, and his oldest son Miles would have to agree. Mae does also but in the

FIG. 5–3 Continued

story she only eludes to this she never talks about it openly. Jesse would love to live forever, he thinks it would be wonderful. However, his family doesn't follow his thinking. Maybe they think so because he is "young," but Tuck brings up a good point in the book when he is talking to Winnie. In chapter 12 he says, "But dying is part of the wheel right next to being born. You can't pick out the pieces you like and leave the rest. Being part of the whole thing, that's a blessing." Miles lost his family because they were in the cycle and he is not. So, being out the cycle brings hurt to you as well. Being in the cycle means you can change, and being out of it means you have to stay the same person forever.

I would not want to die but that would mean living forever and being out the cycle of life. That would mean your not really living, or being human. Being in the cycle means your living, helping the earth from being overpopulated, but it also means that your not being a rock on the side of the stream, as father Tuck puts it. If I had to live forever it would drive me crazy!

The Tuck family has to live forever and living forever is not just a burden, it is a fate worse than death. It doesn't always mean being happy forever. Sure, it might be nice for a while, but then you start to get worried and have to carry around a life-threatening secret. In chapter 12 Tuck says "You can't have living without dying. So you can't call it living, what we got. We just are, we just be, like rocks on the side of the road." I totally agree with Tuck. You can't have living without dying. Everyone has to die at some point in his or her life, so just enjoy what you have, and that will be a life, a **true one.**

FIG. 5–3 *Continued*

from the book. Kayla's letter (Fig. 5–4) shows that Jane's conferring helps Kayla and her partner read their book with a focus.

Teaching Implication

When teaching students to write to prompts on theme or other literary elements, teachers must separate the thinking and talking about the content of the text from instruction on how to write in a genre (e.g., essay, letter); these aspects must be taught separately. The content of what to write is

Dear Mrs. Levy,

The next book Adrianne and I chose to read was Dragon Rider by Cornelia Funke. One of the things we talked about was change. Since Dragon Rider is a fantasy book, it has a lot of change in it. One of the things you talked about with us was the change in Twigleg's feeling. In about a week or so, Twigleg went from cunning and mean to friendly and nicer. We decided that one of the things Cornelia was trying to show you is the friendship difference in Nettle Brand and Firedrake's friends. Firedrake's friends are Sorrel and Ben. I inferred that Twigleg was cunning and mean because he agreed to spy on Firedrake, Ben, and Sorrel. The only time he was ever even slightly nice was when he was with NettleBrand. I inferred that Twigleg turned nicer because he helped save Sorrel from being a science experiment and made jokes frequently. He also started to call Ben young master and he had always called NettleBrand master, so that showed some change. Anyway, this is what we had to say about friendship.

If you are treated badly your whole life you'll act badly and when you are treated better you turn nicer. Friendship has a big influence on people; it is a big part of our lives.

We thought that was good, but we thought there was more behind Twigleg's big change. We also thought his change had to do with his childhood. When Twigleg was extremely young, NettleBrand killed Twigleg's 10 brothers. This is what we said about childhood, even though we didn't have much.

Childhood can really affect your future. It teaches us right from wrong, but sometimes the right from wrong you learn isn't correct.

We soon after figured out that both of these thing had to do with influences. This was our conclusion about influences.

No matter where you go influences are flooding your life. You can work with some, and avoid others, but they are always there.

We continued to trace that thought throughout the book and I thought we did a terrific job. Cornelia Funke is a talented writer and I look forward to re-reading her other books and digging deeper into them. This is probably the most I have ever gotten out of a book in a long time. My notes are in my readers notebook so if you would like to look at them you may. Thank you so much for getting us started on change.

Sincerely,

Kayla Radzvilowicz

FIG. 5–4 *A fifth grader's literary letter about her partnership's assigned topic*

separate from the genre in which to write it (Probst, 2004; Angelillo, 2003a). To teach this, it is important to include the following.

- Use the read-aloud to identify one or two themes that will drive whole-class, small-group, and partner discussions

- Confer with small groups and partnerships to determine whether or what kind of additional teaching is needed

- Use reading workshop to teach engagement with literature

- Design a separate unit of study in writing workshop to teach a genre of essay writing

- Refer back to the content of previous teaching to hold students accountable for ways to talk about assigned topics

- Plan a time in writing workshop to teach a long-term unit of study about writing to prompts

- Plan for units of study in fiction, essay, and other nonfiction writing

Using Prompts Wisely to Get the Most Benefit From Author Studies

Author studies are an excellent way to teach students to know one writer in depth (Jenkins, 1999; Kotch and Zackman, 1995). More important than that, author studies teach students to think across texts and to notice style, craft, and theme within the body of one writer's work and to apply those ways of thinking to other authors. Because the work is so supported by immersion in one author, this is a good opportunity to teach students to think and write about assigned topics. Such assignments often grow naturally from classroom discussions about the author or common threads students discern in all the author's work.

During an author study, it is far less important that students learn a great deal about him or her than that they learn how to study and learn from *any* author. Students can learn to identify the characteristics of an author's writing and to do this in any text or genre. In effect, author study prepares students to respond to prompts about *any* work because it focuses on how to think, study, and write about an author. Teachers build in foundational concepts, which students can use in the next study and the next, that transcend any study (e.g., types of characters the author writes about, big ideas or themes the author considers frequently).

Although it is almost impossible to plan out any unit of study without considering the students, there are broad strokes for teaching the study of an author. Each broad goal would contain within it very specific targeted lessons in varying structures (e.g., whole-class, small-group, individual instruction). The next sidebar contains some broad teaching goals to consider while planning an author study, any of which might become an assigned topic while the class reads a work by the author.

The questions in the sidebar form a good place to begin, and they can apply to any author. So, teachers need not be concerned that students haven't "done" Cynthia Rylant or John Steinbeck because *any* author who

Author Study Teaching Goals to Consider

- Which good writing qualities are well developed in the author's work?

- In what ways does the author "live as a writer" to find writing ideas and to develop them into writing projects?

- What is the author's process for writing, especially for thinking out ideas, planning, researching, and revising?

- How does the author use the writing craft to convey meaning?

- How do life experiences influence the writer's work, especially in terms of professional growth (e.g., writers' groups, editors, mentors), thus teaching students to build an intellectual support community?

- How are themes and ideas examined over and over in the author's work through different plots and characters?

- Which characters and relationships show up often in the author's work?

- What way does the author use language or conventions to tell a story?

- What voice and/or style does the author use?

- How and why does the author choose genres?

- How can author study be generalized to other studies and to writing in a global sense?

has written several texts will be appropriate for this study. Since the work for an author study is highly scaffolded, it is appropriate to use the content to teach students to write to assigned topics.

Several Ways to Organize Author Studies

- The entire class reads different books by the same author and discusses assigned topics across texts (i.e., intertextual study).

- The teacher reads one book by the author aloud while students are reading other books by the same author; this can be organized into book clubs (i.e., assigned topics are based on one aspect of the read-aloud book that students must find in their book club text and write about).

- The teacher's read-aloud books are by one author and they are used to teach many concepts about authors in general; each student studies an author of her or his choice or the book club chooses an author to study (i.e., assigned topics come from the read-aloud books and students transfer them independently to their authors' books).

Conversations become very rich as students are taught intertextuality, and they reinforce concepts of recurring themes and characters. The teaching focuses on many facets from the list of teaching goals (see preceding sidebar) in terms of how students can learn to study all authors through just one.

Author Study Shaped by Assigned Topics

Let's assume a teacher wants to use assigned topics as a way to guide students' understanding of the author study. Within a range of possible topics, students can be offered choice. For example, they can discuss some assigned aspect of character, theme, or setting in their talk groups and then write individually about it. In some cases, teachers want to create a common ground for everyone, so they prefer that students all talk and write about the same topic. *Caution:* Assigning topics must not be the only type of thinking and writing in reading and writing classrooms. It is one way to think, but not the only way. If overdone, use of assigned topics robs students of ownership and self-confidence.

In addition, all students should have the opportunity to talk about any topic before writing, except of course in testing situations. Although testing is examined later in Chapter 9, in most classrooms students must be able to talk before writing in order to clarify their ideas. Teachers may design studies that examine many aspects of an author's work, or they may choose to narrow the study to one or two aspects. Therefore, examining character development or craft (Ray, 1999; Fletcher and Portalupi, 1998; Romano, 2004) in an author study becomes the assigned topic that drives students' work.

When sixth-grade teacher Tina Colangelo teaches her author study of Kevin Henkes, her goal is to teach many ways to revise by studying his writing (Angelillo, 2005). However, she wisely knows that teachers can use one text or group of texts for multiple teaching opportunities. So she extends the Henkes study by asking students to identify themes he tends to write about in his books. The students mention many ideas but eventually distill them down to the following three they think might be in other authors' writing as well.

◈ Growing up means finding your place in the world and growing to love yourself.

◈ You can learn a lot from the grown-ups you know if they are wise and sensitive and you listen carefully.

◈ Families should support and take care of their children's emotional as well as physical needs.

Tina challenges her students to keep those themes in mind as they read other books to see if they come up again. She uses the Henkes study as a way to teach intertextuality; the themes become "assigned topics" for reading of other books. Since universal themes tend to show up again and again, Tina wants students to understand that knowing one author well is a lens with which to study other authors and literature in general. She asks them to write in their notebooks about themes in Henkes' work that appear in other texts; students find similar themes in *The Great Gilly Hopkins*, *Number the Stars*, *Touching Spirit Bear*, *The River Between Us*, *A Long Way to Chicago*, and many other books, as follows.

◈ Families and friends support each other through good times and bad.

◈ People should have confidence in their own abilities.

- It takes courage to face danger, even in the ordinary, daily events of life.

- Change is difficult to get used to, but it is important for growth.

This looking at themes across books becomes the assigned topic for student writing about independent texts, even though it is anchored in the study of Henkes.

This investigation makes Tina and the other sixth-grade teachers in her school think that perhaps students might be taught to investigate several themes thoroughly, in terms of their own lives and the world, and then to look for those themes across literature. Students therefore can enter into reading a book with this thought: "I am going to look at this book in terms of how families support each other through difficulty" or any of a number of other themes. Of course, there are some texts that will not contain a particular theme or it will be a minor part of them. One part of critical reading is to be able to discern the absence of an idea. But students still practice reading "with an angle" and taking an idea from one text to another.

Tina also thinks that the practice of working with one idea, seeing it from multiple perspectives and carrying it into their lives to find richer meaning, over time is beneficial for students. As they work in small groups, she asks her students to think about the idea of family support, but she varies the way they think about the prompt to give them practice in working with an idea that may not always "fit." Her goal is to provide practice with ideas that may seem unusual or unfamiliar to them and to give them opportunities to figure out how they would tackle questions such as the following.

- How would you think about it if it were not a major factor in this book?

- How would you think about it if it wasn't supported by the text at all?

- What would you answer if this were a prompt on the state writing test?

- How would you answer if you had no idea how this prompt fits with this text and you can find no evidence?

- How can your knowledge of the writer's craft, specific authors, elements of story, or themes help you answer?

- How can you use the previous teaching in class to help you answer a prompt?

Teaching Implications

Author studies provide students with a range of learning opportunities, from falling in love with an author to looking across books for themes.

Teachers do their best teaching when they consider how students will use lessons again and again. Assigned topics for thinking, talking, and writing should grow from student work and literature, but they should also point toward larger goals for literacy. The prompt itself should not be the goal but rather a way to spark students' interest in something new or to challenge them to grow new thinking. Assigned topics for author studies do not end when the author's last book is read; they begin at that point by giving students ideas to take with them to the next book and the next author.

Teaching Assigned Writing for Nonfiction Studies

Most teachers now believe that reading and writing nonfiction require discrete skills that must be taught. Too many students cannot read their science texts or understand their math problems for everyone not to realize the reading implications of learning to read nonfiction (Harvey, 1998; McMackin and Siegel, 2002; Robb, 2004). Nonfiction reading and writing is a much bigger teaching issue than writing social studies reports (Robb, 2003); the world of nonfiction is filled with wonderful texts in many genres for students to explore and enjoy (see sidebar). Students often have less choice in content-area work than they have in English class. Reports are assigned and essays are required for unit tests or projects; written interpretations of documents and information are ongoing expectations. I believe students should have greater choice in content areas and applaud districts and teachers who give them choices. However, the same work of engagement with an unfamiliar topic and thinking, talking, and writing about it is as important in content-area work as it is in ELA classes (see Chapter 6 for a description of one teacher who did this study).

Because teachers acknowledge the pervasiveness of writing to prompts, however, they must consider paying more attention to teaching students *how* to think and to write to them. They also must consider the burden of responsibility on them—teachers must write clear, fair, and challenging prompts for all students. To maintain student choice, it is important to offer a variety of assigned topics for classroom work.

Some Rich and Varied Nonfiction Genre Choices

- Articles (feature, news, sports)
- Editorials, letters, essays (personal, persuasive, literary)
- Reviews (books, movies, music, video games)
- Commentaries, profiles, memoirs
- Personal narratives, diaries, autobiographies, biographies
- Directions
- Research reports
- Obituaries
- Weather reports and analyses
- Historical reports

Making the Most of Prompts for Required Projects

The third-grade teachers at one school I visit are planning a unit of study with nonfiction picture books. While they acknowledge that giving students free choice of topic would be preferable, they also know that they have a required science unit on the desert in the curriculum. "How can we get the most mileage from something we have to do anyway?" one of them asks. So they decide to merge the two studies.

Valerie Cavanaugh expresses her concern about teaching students research skills with limited resources on appropriate reading levels. However, all three teachers have many children's books and articles about the desert at various reading levels, and this partially drives their decision to restrict student choice. They therefore decide to ask students to write a picture book about a desert animal. They also know that soon the students will be required to write to a districtwide prompt—"Do you think a hedgehog would make a good pet?"

The teachers hope that thinking and talking about animals for the picture book study will raise students' awareness of animals and of prompt writing. This is the prompt they design to drive their study: "Choose one desert animal to write about in a picture book. Be sure to include interesting and important facts about the animal."

It is agreed that this prompt is less than exciting, but the teachers feel it will get the job done. It will focus students early in the study, it will drive their research, and it will help them differentiate between important and interesting information. In this case, teachers chose to design the prompt because there was so much other teaching they had do in the study (e.g., a sense of nonfiction as a genre, voice and slant in picture books, text layout, nonfiction text features). They focus on teaching students to identify the animal for the books, sharing information with partners, collecting facts and reflecting on them, and talking in groups about each animal and what they want others to remember after reading their books (Harvey, 1998).

The teachers report that the most valuable part of the study, apart from the lovely picture books (see Fig. 5–5) students produce, is the talking and responsive writing students do while researching. These third graders chose their topics within the constraint of desert animals. They did research and worked on the layout of the books. Most important, their teachers taught them that writing to an assigned topic requires saying something new or original about the topic based on what is learned from research. Chapter 8 takes an in-depth look at long-term research projects.

The Red Cobra

By Benjamin Sagalyn   Illustrated by Benjamin Sagalyn

The Red cobra

I dedicate this book to My Dad Michael Sagalyn for keeping me going.

Table of contents

pg1 Chapter one: Is the Red Cobra dangerous?
pg2 Chapter two: whats its Real name?
pg3 Chapter three: length
pg4 Chapter four: location
pg5 five: Hunting
pg7 six: food
pg8 Seven: protecting itself

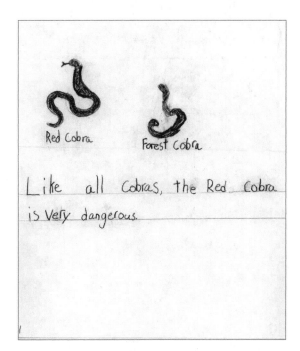

Red Cobra   Forest Cobra

Like all Cobras, the Red Cobra is very dangerous.

FIG. 5–5   A third grader's desert animal picture book

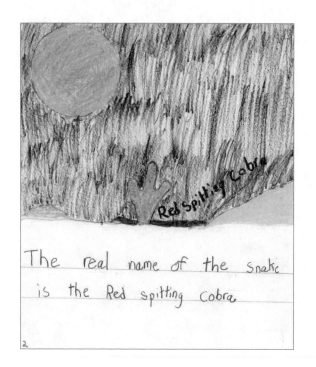

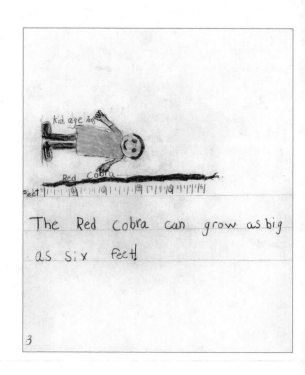

The real name of the snake is the Red spitting cobra.

The Red Cobra can grow as big as six feet.

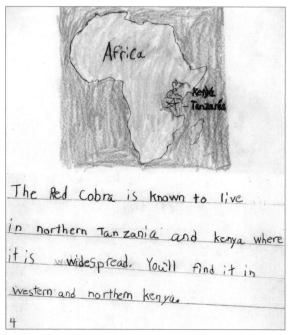

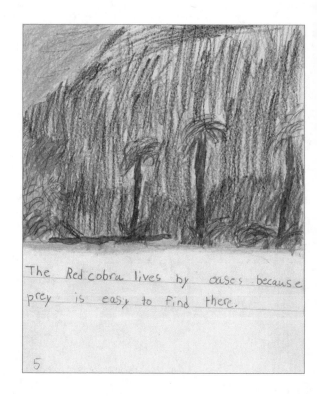

The Red Cobra is known to live in northern Tanzania and kenya where it is widespread. You'll find it in western and northern kenya.

The Red cobra lives by oases because prey is easy to find there.

FIG. 5–5 Continued

The Red cobra is nocturnal. That means it is a night time hunter.

6

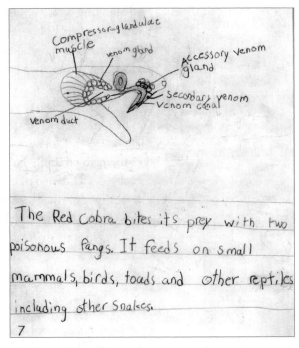

Compressor glandulae muscle
venom gland
Accessory venom gland
Secondary venom
Venom canal
venom duct

The Red Cobra bites it's prey with two poisonous fangs. It feeds on small mammals, birds, toads and other reptiles, including other snakes.

7

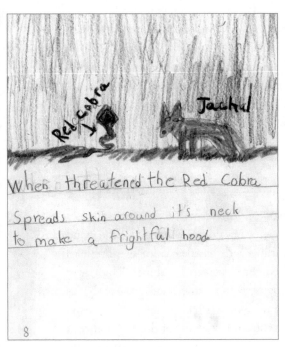

Red Cobra

Jackal

When threatened the Red Cobra spreads skin around it's neck to make a frightful hood.

8

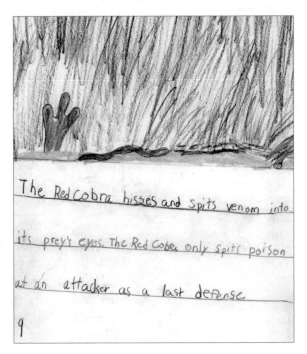

The Red cobra hisses and spits venom into it's prey's eyes. The Red Cobra only spits poison at an attacker as a last defense.

9

FIG. 5–5 Continued

I also work with a group of fourth-grade teachers who are attempting to modify a decades-old "report on the states" that their district requires students to do for social studies. Choosing one of fifty states for their research and writing is the only choice students have for this report. The teachers wisely conclude that the same content work can be accomplished by writing a feature article, although students would still be constrained by the choose-a-state requirement. They read Stephanie Harvey's book *Nonfiction Matters* (1998), Laura Robb's *Nonfiction Writing From the Inside Out* (2004), and the feature article chapter from *The No-Nonsense Guide to Teaching Writing* (2003) by Judy Davis and Sharon Hill. Then the teachers and I plan the unit of study together based on goals they establish: teaching the genre of feature article writing, teaching students to elaborate on their topic, and making their writing interesting.

In each case, the teachers decided to narrow students' choice, partially to ensure success because of limited resources. Some teachers may choose to do this, even though it is always braver and more meaningful to students to write about something they love. Nevertheless, teaching students to wrap their minds around something presents them with a way to exercise their minds, both in the thinking and writing about the idea and in the chance to develop an interest in something new through research and discovery. These teachers also believe that students should have the experience of developing a passion for something in which they may have no interest. It is difficult to like something you know little about, they argue. This type of thinking is, however, often required in the school and work worlds, so they agree to teach the content of the states report as well as the thinking work behind figuring out what is asked in a prompt.

Summary

The most significant part of this work, I think, is to teach students to *glory* in engaging with someone else's ideas or new ideas. There is also the grand satisfaction that comes from wrestling with an idea, from sweating and struggling to figure it out until the light of perception shines. The power and empathy that come from engaging with another's ideas reveal shades of understanding that might remain unknown had someone not offered something else to think about. Teachers rob students of this experience if they do not teach them how to struggle to understand and then to write about that new understanding.

The challenge for teachers is to design work that will raise the bar for all students and to give them the tools to be able to succeed. Thinking, talking, and then writing to prompts must push students in order to engage their curiosity. When they believe that a prompt is just testing their memories or sending them into unnecessary speculation, students may shut down. But prompts that allow students to take some knowledge and work it to create original thinking are worthwhile brain exercise. Teachers can scaffold this by allowing time for reflection, conversation, note-taking, reconsideration, and then writing. The next chapter takes a look at the work one teacher did to teach her writing workshop students to write well to prompts in social studies by having them write about assigned topics for which they had no background knowledge for support.

To Do in Classrooms

- Consider adding writing to prompts in author studies and nonfiction work

- Teach the concept of universal themes that appear in many books; use this as a basis for prompt writing across books

- Continue to use talking and note-taking in partnerships and book clubs to support writing to prompts longer

- Use ongoing observation, conferring, and study of students' readers' notebooks to plan instruction

- Hold students accountable for previous teaching by having them use it to write to prompts

6

What About Your Rights?

Assigned Topics for Content-Area Work

I fell in love with history years after I graduated from college. I had fine teachers in school and a solid curriculum, but the information just didn't light me up. It wasn't the teachers' fault, it was mine. I just didn't care. I had no interest in what dead people had done or why. But sometime in my thirties, I got hooked. How I regret all I missed back in school when I was writing love notes and reading novels in the back of the room. All I can conjure from those days are large maps at the front of dusty rooms, long chapters in textbooks with questions at the end, and multiple-choice tests with the inevitable assigned essays. I'm sure it wasn't that bleak, but to my then adolescent mind, it was, well, mind-numbing.

Later, my sophomore year college history professor gently counseled me. She said that if I didn't see those dead people and long ago events still alive within my soul and my surroundings, I would never catch on. I nearly failed her course. I wish I could tell her now that I eventually did catch on. Today, my kids gag at the thought of going on vacation with me, lest I drag them to another cathedral, battlefield, or restoration.

Many factors caused my young malaise, but I cannot help wondering how much the dreaded assigned topics of those days made me "zone out." The way I was back then is much the same as so many students are today. Now I realize that at the time I didn't know how to engage with an idea, much less with something that had happened decades or centuries ago. A lot of the required writing seemed to test whether I had read the textbook (I hadn't). If the assigned prompts were literal, I was bored. But if they pushed me to interpret information, I probably thought, "How'm I supposed to figure this out?" What was missing in my otherwise fine education that caused me to recoil from content-area prompted writing? Why didn't I hook onto historical or scientific facts and run with, rather than from, them?

Shirley Brice Heath (1987) writes of the oral essay's roots, which she also traces to journals and letters in which people examine and wrestle with ideas and issues on paper. Heath's criticism of school essays is that the entire oral and personal nature of essays is ignored, and therefore the current school essay has little to do with the true nature of an essay. She stresses that students must be taught certain preliminaries before they can write essays. They must retell experiences using evidence, see themselves as "knowers," feel free to express expertise about a body of knowledge, and learn how words are used and language is organized. I suppose I never saw myself as a *knower* or expert on historical or scientific facts. Plus, I had few opportunities to talk about facts using evidence, nor to play with the language of essay as a writer.

Coincidentally, Sarah Daunis, a teacher from a study group I once facilitated, has the same question on her mind when she calls me one Saturday to chat. Her fifth graders are required to take a statewide social studies test that measures students' interpretation of document-based information and their ability to write about it clearly and precisely. The test of course, is prompted writing. Given what we know about the role of conversation in shaping student work, Sarah and I decide to apply this concept to her social studies curriculum. As an outgrowth of that, this chapter takes a look at the content-area work of talking about facts and ideas and writing the essay.

Talking About Facts and Ideas

From the first day of school, Sarah establishes reading and writing workshops in her classroom. She focuses on assessing students' needs, and along with studying the curriculum calendar of her school, she makes decisions about whole-class, small-group, and individual instruction. A unit of study in reading and writing nonfiction is already part of her yearly plan, but Sarah decides to also bring the nonfiction work into the social studies part of her day so that the thinking, talking, and writing extends to content-area work.

After meeting to plan our work, we decide to focus on teaching Sarah's students to talk about a familiar topic for a while. Starting with their notebooks, we ask them to find an entry in their writers' notebooks that they can talk about for five minutes. We do this to help them understand that often people have to talk (or write) about something when they think there is little more to say, and that there are ways to push ourselves to say more. In her lesson, Sarah demonstrates that she forces herself to say more about her own notebook entry by thinking of an emotion that is attached to the experience. Her students practice talking using their own entries and then together build a chart of strategies they can use to make themselves talk longer. Sarah and I notice that students generally can talk about familiar topics from their notebooks; however, we know that assigned topics are often unfamiliar to students. This is especially prevalent on statewide exams, like the ones Sarah's students must take. So we decide to work with them on making someone else's topic their own.

Making Someone Else's Topic Your Own

I visit Sarah's classroom so that she and I can *fishbowl*—model—a conversation that consists of each of us assigning a topic to the other. We choose topics that we know are unfamiliar to each other, but from which we can model hooking one's mind into an idea. We rehearse our performance ahead of time because we want to be sure to demonstrate certain points (see sidebar). This kind of practice ensures that we will teach exactly what we want students to learn.

On the day of the lesson, Sarah scans her notebook and stops at one page. Then she says to me, "I have an entry I wrote when my husband Matt broke his ankle. So, Janet, talk to me about that."

I squirm in my chair. "Gee, Sarah, I don't know anything about your husband breaking his ankle."

Sarah smiles. "I know that. But what could you say about it if you *had* to talk about it?" Sarah's class sits forward in anticipation. I can almost hear them wondering how I'm going to get out of this predicament. How *do* you talk about something you know or care little about?

I clear my throat. "Well, I guess I could talk about the time I broke my hand and how much it hurt. I could tell you how it happened, or the hospital visit, or about how hard it was to do anything for weeks after that. I could relate that to Matt by imagining that he had the same feelings and experiences."

Sarah turns to the chart paper beside her. "Good. You could make yourself talk about it by remembering when a similar event happened to you." She writes my strategy on the chart. "But what if you had never broken your hand? What would you do then?"

"Oh gee," I say. "I guess that's true. We can't all have had every experience or know something about everything. I guess I could tell you about when my daughter broke her wrist. Of course, it would sound different, because it would be about my distress as her mom, but I could draw from that. It would have a different perspective, but I could do it."

Sarah adds that strategy to the chart. "Okay, but what if you never knew anyone who had broken any bones?" The class giggles. They are used to Sarah raising the bar to force them to think, and they enjoy watching her challenge me.

"I guess then I could think back to books I've read or movies I've seen or stories people have told me as a way to talk about it."

Sarah smiles. "Good job." Then we both laugh.

It's my turn now. I ask Sarah to talk about the New York Yankees. She laughs, because she's a Boston Red Sox fan. So she talks about the Yankees in terms of the damage they've done to Boston's World Series dreams over the years. Sarah turns to the class and says:

> Sometimes you have to talk or write about something you know very little about, and that can make you feel nervous or worried. But using the strategies that Janet and I just demonstrated, you can figure out ways to do it. This is important because sometimes on a test, there is a question that seems unfamiliar, and I want you to be able to deal with that. Today I'd like you to work in partnerships and assign each other topics from your notebooks to talk about. Then I want you to use the strategies on the chart to push yourself to talk about your partner's topic for three minutes.

Sarah and I listen to students' partnership conversations. We agree that some students talk with ease and others clearly need help. This is important for us to know because these same students might become upset or angry if they have no strategies for answering an unfamiliar prompt. We know students need more practice doing this.

The following is a transcript of a brief student conversation on the assigned topic of baseball. Notice how Arushi uses several moves to support Brittany.

ARUSHI: I like baseball *(starts by stating opinion)*

BRITTANY: I don't like baseball. *(counteropinion; possible attempt to shut topic down)*

ARUSHI: Do you watch baseball? *(attempt to develop partner's personal connection to topic)*

BRITTANY: No. *(doesn't use strategy to engage)*

ARUSHI: Do you know some players? Have you read any books or articles about players? *(trying to build some way to talk about topic)*

BRITTANY: *(shrugs)* No. I told you I don't like it.

ARUSHI: So you're saying you don't know anything at all about baseball? Not even what other people say about it? *(challenging partner to figure out a way to connect)*

BRITTANY: Yeah, okay. So I hear my brother talk about it sometimes.

ARUSHI: Okay, so let's talk about what some people think about baseball.

Through negotiation, the students finally find a common ground to talk about a topic about which they actually know very little.

When we debrief after class, Sarah decides her work for the next week is to help students build confidence in their ability to talk about others' ideas. She also plans to ask them to write about each other's ideas (see Fig. 6–1).

The next time I visit, Sarah takes me aside with a concern. "Aziz is a bright and conscientious student. But when his partner asked him to write about cats, he was so frustrated that he crumpled up his paper and threw it away." She shows me the wrinkled sheet. "I fished it out of the garbage." She shakes her head. "If Aziz could get so upset about having to write about an unfamiliar topic, imagine what could happen to some of the others on the day of the test. This tells me that this work is even more important than I thought."

More than ever, Sarah and I want to build students' strength for taking on an idea and having confidence to think and write about it. She and I talk at length about the gaming skills we know students have and are convinced that there is much to learn from that. James Gee says that students should be "using technology, texts, and games in an integrated way" (2003, 23) so that they learn "to think reflectively and actively about connections between texts, activities and the world" (Norton-Meier, 2005, 430). We

Kassandra Patraju assigned me to write
about Ripley's Believe it or Not!

Aziz Al-Yami
Ripley's Believe it or Not!   10|2|

     I don't know much about
Ripley's Believe it or Not! But Kassandra
Patraju does, she has the book and
she has been to the museum itself!
Surprisingly, Kassandra says the book
is more exciting than the museum, which
was actually the opposite of what she
had expected at first. (I would
think so too!)
     While I can't say much about
Ripley's Believe it or Not, I can make
many comparisons to how Kassandra
expected the museum to be better than
the book, which turned out not to
be true, in her opinion. One
comparison, for example, would be
the time I bought a video game
called "Megaman Battle Network 4".
There are two different versions of
this game, "Blue Moon" and "Red
Sun". I bought both, and expected
Blue Moon to be better, since it
seems the majority of people in the
world like the color blue more than
red. But after playing both of the games,
I enjoyed "Red Sun" a lot more than
"Blue Moon". I have many other
examples of me expecting something to be
better than something else, but it turns
out it isn't. Too bad I don't have
time to explain them all...

               By Aziz Al-Yami

FIG. 6–1 *Examples of students' writing done to prompts assigned by partners*

Date | Genre | Pg # | Entry
10/21 | Non-fiction | 34 | 21

H.W

What I Know about Cats
By Nora Giblin Allison Weiser

Cats are very hard to take care of. first you have to give them food. Cats should get food in the morning and in the evening. Second is the poop. Every time there is poop in the "litter you should clean it up. If you don't Pe-U. Thridly you should play with your cat utherwise they won't feel safe with you. That's how my cat feels. Forthly you should give your cat water or else it will get dehidrated. The last thing you should do is get a cat if you don't have one.

FIG. 6-1 Continued

Aziz Al-Yami
Ripley's Believe it or Not!

Kassandra Patraju assigned me to write about

10/21/04

Kassandra	Aziz
-Has seen show that is about unusual things	-Heard of Ripley's never read book or went there
-Has a book about it	-Hasn't ever seen weird things like the ones in Ripley's
-Only time she saw such weird things in her own eyes was in a museum	-Want's to go to Ripley's
	-Will get the book
	-I don't know anything
	-Doesn't have anything to say about Ripley's

Essay.

Nora's story

<u>Topic :</u>
<u>Driving when</u>
<u>5 years old</u>

. Driving when 5 years old
. Turned the wheel to much
. Coming back from sesame place

<u>Relations :</u>

. When about 6 years old <u>I</u> kind of drove, but my dad held the wheel
. This was in the Philippines
. Going back to house

Essay   10/21

<u>Driving</u>

   When it was sunset one day when I was about 6 years old my dad asked, "Jayson, do y want to try driving."
   "Okay," I answered though I was scared to do it, but I wanted to, like the way Nora felt when she tried to drive for the first time, felt the same way as me. It was a very simular story because both of us found out that even though you think you don't want to do something you can still do it. In the end nothing bad happened to me, but in Nora's situation she turned the car to the side to much, but the point is even though she was scared and I was scared we both still wanted to do it

FIG. 6–1 *Continued*

know that using connections between texts, outside activities, and what they know of the world can support students' written responses to any question.

We recognize another concern as well. Talking and writing flatly about a topic does not indicate thorough intellectual engagement any more than nonchalantly pushing game-controller buttons indicates involvement in a video game. We know that writers find their voices while writing about a topic and then use their voice to show passion for the topic (Romano, 2004). So we agree that, at some point, we will not only teach students to take on others' ideas but to use writers' tools (e.g., voice, word choice) to make their writing reflect their thinking about the topic (see Chapter 7).

Moving into Social Studies Topics

At the same time that the students have been practicing talking and writing about each other's ideas, Sarah has been teaching the content of her social studies curriculum. Admittedly, it is filled with huge amounts of information, and there are some important concepts in it: human and legal rights in the United States, the history of the struggle for freedom, and the marvelous concept and challenge of democracy as a system of government. It is a large body of information for ten-year-olds, however, and Sarah expects her students to be engaged with all of it.

She tells her class that she wants to extend the thinking and talking work they did when assigning each other topics to working in partnerships to think and talk about new ideas. Sarah assigns the class a social studies topic to talk about and tells them to think about the intellectual moves they make in order to talk, as well as the information they talk about. Reminding students to refer to a copy of the document she has on a chart, the topic she assigns for discussion is: "How did the Declaration of Independence affect the daily lives of the colonists?"

As we listen to students talk, Sarah and I are interested in the ways they figure out *how to answer* the question. For now, we are less concerned about "correct" answers than we are about students' intellectual moves. As we scuttle around the room, we see and hear students doing the following.

- Negotiating and questioning

- Making their thinking grow in order to continue talking

- Stating opinions and making conjectures

- Referring to facts

I specifically listen to a conversation between Christopher, Taiki, and Kevin. They make several interesting moves in addition to those just listed. The boys start by situating themselves in the prompt and thinking how the Declaration affects us now. While they are a few centuries off, they are getting their minds going with the idea that this document changes lives. They state facts they know about the Declaration and define them by saying, "So that means that . . ." They clarify what they say, and several times they disagree. At one point, Taiki helps Christopher find a word ("massacre") he needs and corrects a misconception about the Declaration. They mull over some facts about taxes and monarchy, correct their information by checking the chart, and revise their thinking—"Wait, I take that back. That can't be true."

Kassandra and Tringa decide that when they think they're done talking, that's when they've just gotten to a good idea they can zero in on. They lift their work toward finding significance and how questions come up from talking about a topic. They also refer to facts about the Declaration that they've written in their notebooks and try to figure out which facts they can use and which are extraneous. What fascinates me about their conversation is their insight—often we suddenly understand new depths of a topic to plumb just when we think we're done with it! I think back on Don Murray's often quoted question, "How do I know what I think until I see what I write?" And I think, "How do I know how my thinking is moving until I hear what I say?" Kassandra and Tringa figure out what they are thinking by reflecting on what they've said and by understanding that thinking is recursive.

Fig. 6–2 shows some of the ways Sarah's students engage with the topic she assigned and move into partner conversations. The following excerpt shows one student using questions to prod her partner to talk about the topic.

AZRA: Okay, so the question is to think about the Declaration and how it affected the colonists. (*restating question*)

MORGANA: I studied the Constitution. (*making attempt to use prior knowledge*)

AZRA: The Constitution doesn't have anything to do with this. What do you think about the Declaration of Independence? (*clarifying and pulling back to topic*)

MORGANA: It was good, because then they didn't have to do what somebody else said. (*trying to understand implications*)

- Start with something basic you notice and build off that idea

- Try to build a line of thinking, such as how it affected food supply or safety

- Talk about your opinion and support it

- Listen to partner to hear other perspectives

- Ask questions: Do you remember . . . ? What do you think of . . . ? Why do you think that . . . ? When did that happen . . . ?; use facts and evidence as support

- Speak from your passions and interests

- Allow your thinking to flow

- Connect to yourself and then go back to the time period and the text

- State facts and explain them

- Clarify, negotiate, disagree

- Help each other find the right word

- Rethink ideas

- Go back and zoom in on one aspect of the topic

- Ask, "So what?" then find significance

- Try to fit other information to it

- Recognize when new questions arise

- Think of similarities and differences

- Focus on one thing and build off it

- Connect to another time

- Come to some conclusions

FIG. 6–2 *Responding to and interacting with someone else's social studies topic*

AZRA: So that means you think they didn't want to do what anybody else said? (*restating what someone said*)

MORGANA: Yeah, the king. They didn't want to have to obey the king.

AZRA: Okay. But I'm trying to figure out why that's so important. Who cares about the king? (*looking for significance*)

MORGANA: Because then England would still be ruling us and we would have a king instead of a president. (*drawing conclusion as a result*)

The work of talking and writing about others' ideas continues in Sarah's room for two to three weeks. She requires the conversations and subsequent writing to become longer as students build stamina and practice ways to engage with their partners' ideas. Again and again Sarah confers with students to be sure they understand the thinking moves behind the work—she wants them to know how to engage with an idea and run with it, regardless of familiarity. And she knows that familiarity with an idea comes from letting it roll around in one's mind. Reflection is one way for students to bring their voices to their writing (more about this in Chapter 7), but audience is critical as well. Sarah knows her students will not do their best writing if they do not have enough information or an authentic audience for their writing, someone more immediate than the state writing assessors, whoever they are. So without killing their voices and hoping to teach them that essays have an audience, Sarah moves into the writing work to teach them how to write in the content-area essay genre.

Moving into Writing Workshop

Following the work of talking about and writing in their notebooks on peer-assigned topics, Sarah moves the study to writing workshop. She wants her students to write fine essays that demonstrate their ability to engage with topics and to use evidence to support their thinking. So she designs a writing workshop unit of study to teach them to write essays based on content-area material. As a class, students came up with a chart of elements for a social studies essay (see Fig. 6–3).

While assessing what her students know about essay writing, Sarah concludes that they have little problem with the traditional five-paragraph essay. Its form is simplistic and somewhat stifling compared to the sophisticated thinking they are now able to do (Fig. 6–4). In fact, she finds that while they can write the five-paragraph variety with ease, some essays are flat and lack reflection, as if students know their only requirement is to spit back information in a certain order. Her conclusion is that she must challenge them to be both better thinkers and better writers.

When asked to write a five-paragraph essay, students intuit that they are merely fulfilling an assignment. They often recoil from the rigid, artificial formula that requires strict adherence to form and mock-academic style. The formula—plug in this sentence here and that sentence there—actually mocks students' intelligence because it does not give them the opportunity to play with ideas and unfold their thinking. In fact,

Elements of a Social Studies Essay

➤ Identify text structure to help write your essay
➤ Introduction with line of thought
➤ All bullets are covered in body paragraphs
➤ Indent paragraphs and check spelling
➤ Can use own background information
➤ Stay on topic and be specific
➤ Real, accurate and important facts from documents
➤ Reread to make sure it makes sense
➤ Conclusion with lesson

FIG. 6–3 *Students' list of elements for a social studies essay*

five-paragraph essays are just too easy and simplistic for students; they can do much more. There's little place for the students as writers and thinkers in this type of essay—it's impersonal and stifling. If teachers are honest with themselves, they'll ask whether this is the type of writing—dry, dull, dusty—they want to teach students.

Tom Romano says, as an English teacher, it's not the sort of writing he wants to spend his one wild and precious life reading. It has no "currency" beyond the classroom (2004, 61–62). So teachers must ask:

◈ Is this all we want them to know about expository writing when they graduate?

◈ Is this all we have to teach them about jousting with a grand idea or fascinating facts?

◈ Is this the best we can do to teach the beauty and power of the essay?

It's little wonder so many adults do not see themselves as writers. If this is what they were taught in school, no wonder they flee from writing.

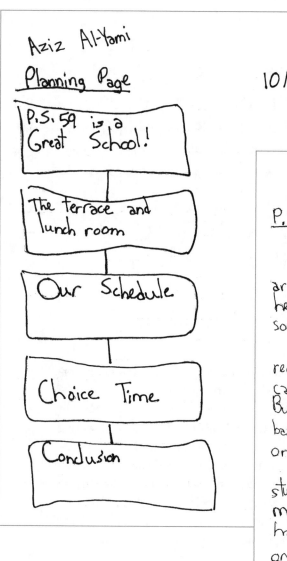

Aziz Al-Yami

Planning Page   10/22

P.S. 59 is a
Great School!

The Terrace and
lunch room

Our Schedule

Choice Time

Conclusion

FIG. 6–4 *Aziz's essay about PS 59*

10/22

P.S. 59 is a Great School!

   P.S. 59 is a great school! There
are so many awesome things we do
here! We have math, reading, writing,
social studies and other cool subjects!
   Every day we have lunch and
recess at 12:15 P.M. At lunch we
can have home lunch or school lunch.
But recess is awesome! We can play
basketball, soccer, kickball, football, or go
on our junglegym!
   Our schedule is usually social
studies and reading and math in the
morning. After that we often
have more reading and about
one hour of writing. What we
have after that is random, but
then we have lunch and recess.
We often have social studies, or
shared text after. Then we'll have
either science, music, reading
workshop or choice time depending
on the day. Then we go home!

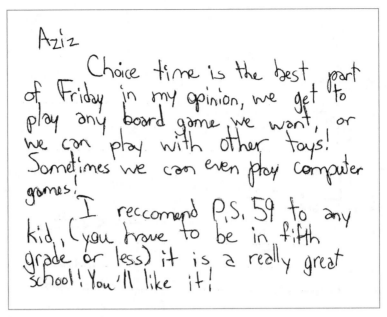

Aziz

Choice time is the best part of Friday in my opinion, we get to play any board game we want, or we can play with other toys! Sometimes we can even play computer games! I reccomend P.S. 59 to any kid, (you have to be in fifth grade or less) it is a really great school! You'll like it!

FIG. 6-4 *Continued*

Romano says the "five-paragraph 'you-know-what' and the sterile, formal, and abstract notions of academic writing that go with it can be killers and lead writers to all kinds of bad habits" (2004, 60). In fact, this school exercise does little to promote or prove good writing or good thinking. Teachers would do well to remember the exhortations on the essay of James Moffett (1983), Randy Bomer (1995), and Tom Romano (2004): It should offer writers the best opportunity to use deep thought, language, craft, wit, and voice to take the reader along on a journey of thought. As teachers, we can make the essay a vibrant expression of intellectual thought, not a strict recipe for cookie-cutter writing.

Teachers who tell me their students "can't write anything better" need to seriously examine what they themselves know about writing the essay and what they've been taught. In his 1989 book, Donald Graves says:

The roots of the effective essay, a sense of point of view, and the development of more advanced communication are in strong, oral discussion, with the addition of ample opportunity for many types of writing. . . . Methods that prescribe form are suspect. Form should follow function, and function is determined by the present-tense orientation of literate events (57).

I recommend reading multiple issues of *The Best Essays* of whatever year to get a flavor of the essay as intellectual play. I firmly believe too that the best essay answers to prompted tests are not formulaic, but filled with depth, voice, and originality.

Sarah recognizes this. She knows her students can do much more, so she challenges herself as a writer. We've worked together so long that she knows I believe in teachers' writing as a powerful model. Therefore, using an essay she has written as a mentor text for the whole class, she asks the class to notice features in her essay.

Students use what they notice from Sarah's essay as a way to build community agreement on what they need to include in an essay. They decide that Sarah's essay introduces her line of thought and engages her readers with the topic. Bulleted facts from Sarah's notebook appear in the inside paragraphs of her essay and she does not include every fact. Sarah stays on her topic and uses background information to make it interesting, but she also uses accurate information from the document. Her conclusion is critical: Students notice that she has used the information to come to a new understanding, and that her conclusion contains an insight or lesson rather than mere restatement of the original idea.

From what the class noticed, Sarah and I make a chart for students to use as they write their own essays. We remind them that Sarah is preparing them for a timed-test experience by slowing the process down and teaching them each step of the way. The major difference between this unit of study and a traditional one is that in this case, Sarah *assigns the topic*. She believes in student choice with evangelical zeal, but for this unit, Sarah is teaching students a discrete skill—answering an essay prompt. Her procedure repeats the original work of talking and writing about a partner's topic, but now it's about the teacher's social studies topic: "Explain the importance of the Iroquois culture." Next, the class holds a group getting-ready-to-write conversation to share any background information about the Iroquois culture.

General Outline for a Writing Workshop Unit of Study

It is important for the teacher to model each step for students using her or his own notebook and writing an essay along with them.

Week One: Immerse students in the genre and identify features of the text; students should continue to gather entries in writers' notebooks.

Week Two: Students identify mentor texts after which they will model their work; students need to choose a topic from their notebooks and gather information on it.

Week Three: Students reread notes and reflections and write a draft, then begin applying revision techniques.

Week Four: Revision continues based on assessment of work, knowledge of qualities of good writing, and the use of mentor texts.

Week Five: Students complete the unit by editing, proofreading, publishing, and reflecting.

NORA: The clan mother is interesting and important.

NICOLE: The Iroquois had relationships and peace.

CHLOE: They had inventory and trading.

TRINGA: They had peace with each other.

ALEXANDER: They lived in long houses.

NIKITA: Generations lived together and would teach kids to do certain things at certain ages.

After students have shared whatever they know about the Iroquois, they are asked to take notes and reflect on their information. She teaches them that it is not enough to state facts, but that they must use the information to show insight into the culture. Students do this by connecting the Iroquois to their own lives, to the beginnings of the country, and to other cultures they have studied. Then Sarah discusses the following and works with them on their actual writing.

* Introductions state the assigned topic and some idea or opinion about it.

* Supporting information is chosen to advance the writer's opinion or idea.

* Conclusions state new insights the writer has come to or leave the reader with something to think about.

Writing the Content-Area Essay

As a reader, I have come to love the essay genre for its sense of intimacy between the writer and readers. The more essays I read, the more I see how essayists allow everyone into their thought processes. The best ones do indeed take readers on a "journey of thought," as if their ideas were unfolding to lead them along. In many ways, reading essays is like reading stories; the end is not apparent while reading, though the writer is moving the reader in a logical direction.

When teaching fiction writing, students are taught to withhold information and reveal it gradually. They understand that plot is centered on a rising tension that grabs hold of readers' minds and pulls them along. This very concept—the deliberate unfolding of information along a continuum toward clarity and climax—is what makes essays interesting, even compelling, to read. Readers enter the reading of an essay with the expectation that they will go on an intellectual ride with the writer as she or he wrestles with a concept and together they will arrive at the end both wiser and renewed.

Once again, teachers face the paradigm shift from students writing essays to prove that they know the information to writing essays to demonstrate their capacity for unfolding thought. With the demands of twenty-first century literacy, the level of teaching must be raised beyond the simple spitting back of information.

Parts of the Essay

Let's agree to use the metaphor of a journey with students while teaching them to write the essay. Journeying requires preparation, planning, embarking, solving problems along the way, enjoyment, and arrival. A journey of thought is much the same thing: The student has or is given an idea, prepares for the journey, embarks on it, experiences turns and twists along the way, and finally arrives at a destination of insight and understanding. Therefore, the parts of an essay can be framed in the following ways: the introduction is the preparation for the journey, what teachers call *the body* is the journey itself, and the conclusion is the destination (see Table 6–1).

Sarah teaches her students the concept of a journey by asking them to record their thinking each step of the way as they talk about the topic. She asks them to stop and jot "What do I think now?" at several points along the way and to reread what they've written to reflect on how their thinking is growing and changing. Since they've had practice kneading an idea from their work on assigning each other topics, students are able to do this. The main challenge is getting them to record their thinking along the way because they are often heading toward "getting" the answer so that they can write the essay. Sarah's point is that she is interested in their thinking as much as the information they've gathered—being able to think about an idea and trace that thinking is more important than knowing any one set of facts. In the end, Sarah's students produce both notes and essays about the prompt that assure her they will be able to write well on the state exam as well as on future assigned content-area topics (see Fig. 6–5).

TABLE 6–1 The Essay Framed as a Journey of Thought

Journey Stages	Part of the Essay	Skills Required

Preparing for the journey—deciding what is needed and the probable destination	*Introduction*—indicates understanding of the prompt; takes a stance on the prompt; surprises and intrigues the reader by withholding information; holds promise for the reader that the journey will be interesting	• Reread to clarify what the prompt is asking
		
		• Engage with the idea of the prompt
		
		• Use internal dialogue if there is no opportunity for conversation
		
		  —What do I know?
		
		  —What facts do I have that relate?
		
		  —What is my slant on this?
		
		  —How can I talk back to this prompt?

Going on the journey—includes waiting, traveling, possible changes in plans, moving from place to place, expecting surprise and fun	*The journey of thought*—weaving facts and reflections or observations to advance the idea; using paragraphs to chunk ideas and cluster facts; arranging facts and/or events to move reader along; equals surprise and movement	• Ability to put facts into logical order • Ability to use facts as landmarks with transitions between them • Understand how facts fit together as milestone markers on the journey to a new place of understanding
Arriving at the destination—reaching apparent end of the journey	*Conclusion*—thinking arrives at a new place, although it is possible to have a sense that the journey isn't completely over but will continue another time; may be more surprises or thinking and reflection; the revelation after the journey is done leaves the reader with some thoughts or insights to contemplate	• Achieve insight or original thinking about prompted idea • Let go of idea after thorough investigation of it • Respect the intelligence and efforts of readers

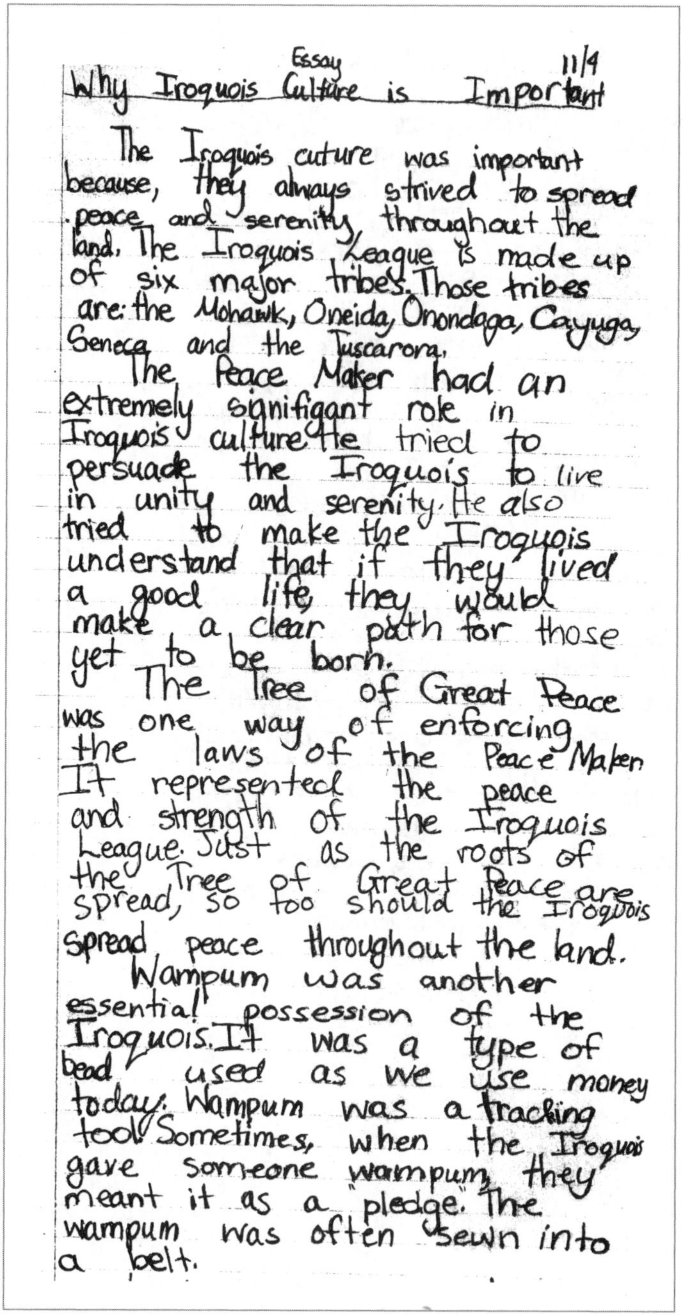

Essay 11/4
Why Iroquois Culture is Important

The Iroquois cuture was important because, they always strived to spread peace and serenity throughout the land. The Iroquois League is made up of six major tribes. Those tribes are: the Mohawk, Oneida, Onondaga, Cayuga, Seneca and the Tuscarora.

The Peace Maker had an extremely significant role in Iroquois culture. He tried to persuade the Iroquois to live in unity and serenity. He also tried to make the Iroquois understand that if they lived a good life, they would make a clear path for those yet to be born.

The Tree of Great Peace was one way of enforcing the laws of the Peace Maker. It represented the peace and strength of the Iroquois League. Just as the roots of the Tree of Great Peace are spread, so too should the Iroquois spread peace throughout the land.

Wampum was another essential possession of the Iroquois. It was a type of bead used as we use money today. Wampum was a tracking tool. Sometimes, when the Iroquois gave someone wampum, they meant it as a "pledge." The wampum was often sewn into a belt.

FIG. 6–5 *Students' social studies essays on assigned topic*

Longhouses served as living quarters for several related Iroquois families. Each family had their own living space and storage area. Although the families lived together, they also had their primary. In longhouses Iroquois families lived in unity.

The Iroquois bands had a Grand Council made up of men and women. The women had "important roles because the "clan mother" chose male members to serve on the Grand Council. The males chose the "sachem" (leader) of the Grand Council. The males also settled disputes by deciding on peaceful solutions.

In Conclusion, all the documents (1-6) of the Iroquois was about being peaceful and trustworthy. I learned, that the same things my family encourage me to practice today, are the very same things the Iroquois have been teaching their people.

FIG. 6–5 *Continued*

<u>Essay</u>

Nov. 4

There were many different tribes in the United States a long time ago. Six of the tribes in parts of New York State made up the culture group, the Iroquois. The Iroquois were important because they had to live together and be honest to each other. The Iroquois were a community of people.

About 400 years ago, Deganawida, the Peace Maker, urged the six tribes to live together as a community. The Peace Maker made thirteen laws, including "peace and unity," to be followed by the group. The Peace Maker also said not to be selfish and always look out for the for the whole group.

Hiawatha, another leader, helped spread the Peace Makers teaching to the tribes and together they formed the Iroquois league. The Peace Maker planted a white pine tree, as a symbol of the union. The Tree of Great Peace represented peace and strength to the Iroquois league.

The Iroquois used wampum beads as money, to trade for goods. We now use

FIG. 6–5 Continued

money to pay for things, such as food. Wampum could be given as a pledge. The giver would promise to live up to an agreement. Most of the time the wampum beads were sewn onto "wampum belt."

In the Iroquois culture, related families lived in longhouses together. The families would have their own living space, cooking fire, and storage place, but it was all an open area. The families seemed very honest and they didn't steal each others thing. If they did, it would have been impossible to live together.

The women and men both had important roles in the Iroquois culture. The women had to chose a clan mother and the clan mother had to chose a clan man to serve on the Grand Council. In the Grand Council, the men chose a leader. They discussed disputes and decied on peace loving solutions.

The Iroquois worked together to build a living community, for it's people. Even though they were from different tribes, the Iroquois people had leaders like Deganawida and Hiawatha to guide them in living peacefully. I hope that one day, even though we are different people from all over the world, we will have some good leaders to lead us to live peacefully and unselfishly.

FIG. 6-5 Continued

Summary

Students need opportunities to practice engaging with others' ideas before they can begin answering prompts about content-area work. Although there needs to be many opportunities to learn facts about various material, students must talk about and negotiate facts' meaning. Teaching that focuses on modeling essays as journeys for readers are interesting to write and compelling to read. For students to understand that events from long ago or facts from science are very much entwined with their day-to-day lives, teachers need to give them opportunities to talk, think, and then write about a variety of content areas.

To Do in Classrooms

- Model with another adult how you get yourself to say something about a completely foreign topic

- Chart strategies for stretching thinking

- Assign social studies or science topics for students to talk and write about

- Teach the essay in writing workshop as a genre of writing and a journey of thought

- Avoid formulas for writing that devalue students' abilities and creativity

7

The Writer's Job
Assigned Topics and the Qualities of Good Writing

One of the things writing teachers fear most is students who forget or choose to ignore all the good teaching and learning about the qualities of good writing when they move from writing about topics of their choice to assigned topics. This mirrors what Julia Cameron says: When we write, something must be at stake, and writers must care about their topics (2000). Often, however, all that is at stake is a grade and students care little about the assigned topic. If they have no "zest for what they are writing about," William Zinsser (1998b, 3) counsels, the writing is in danger of being flat, monotonous, boring. See the students writing just the facts, ma'am. See the teacher reading many papers. See the teacher falling asleep.

I began keeping a journal regularly in college. I liked to reread it, especially when it held the details of a particular event or my growing sense of myself as a feminist and a woman. But even when I was passionate about a topic, as I was in those days about almost everything from war to romantic entanglements, my passions rarely came through in my writing. I simply reported events. Later, on my own, I discovered that when I paid little attention to the *way* I was writing, it made for eye-drooping reading. In other words, all that I didn't know about the qualities of good writing made my writing suffer. True, the topics were important to me. I just didn't "get" that qualities of good writing must drive *all* writing, not just the stuff that one hopes to publish, or texts we read and wish we had written. In fact, I confess I knew little about the qualities of good writing—no voice, no narrative, no careful word choice. Complete sentences and correct spelling—that was what I thought made up good writing.

Today in writing workshop classrooms, teachers model good writing for students by naming and teaching its qualities: ideas, word choice, sentence fluency, conventions, voice, and so on (Anderson, 2005; Spandel, 2000; Culham, 2003; Fletcher and Portalupi, 2001). Students are lucky to have this caliber of writing instruction. As part of the process approach to writing, it is more meaningful for creating good writers than grammar exercises in isolation, which I received in school (Noden, 1999; Weaver, 1996; Ehrenworth and Vinton, 2005). Although there are several different "takes" on what the qualities of good writing are, all of which are valuable, I will add my own list as we examine teaching qualities and assigned topics. The key is to teach that assigned writing can and must have voice, organization, appropriate word choice, and so on, because that is the writer's job, no matter what the topic is.

Qualities of Good Writing
• Solid ideas
• Focus
• Word choice
• Sentence flow
• Written conventions
• Voice
• Organization
• Elaboration

I am convinced that for any type of writing to be successful, writers must pay attention to the qualities of good writing. This chapter examines how to teach those qualities in the context of assigned topics, teaching qualities of good writing all year long, and transferring qualities of good writing from self-chosen to assigned topics.

Teaching the Qualities of Good Writing

Effective writing workshops offer students the best chance for developing skill as writers and for experiencing the power and pleasure of writing. Additional benefits of daily writing workshop include a growing sense of identity as writers; confidence to choose topics from one's life and find significance and meaning in them; and practice in developing a highly sophisticated, demanding, and necessary skill. Essentially, the purpose of writing workshop is to create writers who can write well in any situation and in any genre.

No matter what other demands the curriculum imposes, teachers must always hold the qualities of good writing as the foundation for writing instruction. Therefore, whatever the district requires—reports, essays, fiction stories, poetry, and so on—ongoing instruction in the qualities of good writing will support students' learning and ensure that their writing gets better. In other words, teach qualities of good writing in every unit of study and expect students to carry what they've studied and practiced previously to subsequent units.

In his wonderful book, *What a Writer Needs*, Ralph Fletcher notes that "no element of writing can exist in isolation. . . . Every part, every *word*, depends on its relationship to the whole" (1992, 4). Considering each element separately is by definition artificial, but it is one way to look at how writers put together discrete parts to form an organic whole. Study of the qualities of good writing shifts the writer from fulfilling an assignment imposed from the outside to reaching inside to write for an authentic audience. It signals stepping out of the ego to show respect for the readers of the writing. So, in some ways, attention to the qualities of good writing when writing on assignment shows the writer's maturity; it is a generous move toward the reader.

In addition to all this, writers rehearse and plan writing all the time (Murray, 2003). For one hour of actual writing, writers sometimes rehearse and revise in their minds for hours, living with their topics throughout their days (and sometimes nights). Students who keep writers' notebooks and regularly practice the qualities of good writing—just as musicians who work on notes and scales—become more likely to write well all the time, as well as on an assignment.

Because it is impossible to teach everything in every unit of study, it makes sense to determine which qualities of writing are best taught in each unit. For example, a poetry unit is perfect for studying word choice and language (Flynn and McPhillips, 2000; Heard, 1989). When you write a five-hundred page novel, you can waste a few words; not so with poetry—every word, every nuance of meaning matters. What better place to teach this to students, and *from that time forward*, in every other writing genre, hold them accountable for careful, thoughtful word choices. For other units of study, other qualities can be highlighted, always helping students to understand that regardless of genre, attention to specific qualities unifies and strengthens all writing.

This foundation for writing instruction provides an effective and solid basis for teaching decisions; in each unit of study, decide which qualities of good writing to teach so that all instruction is connected by a continuing thread throughout the year. No matter which genre of writing teachers focus on, or whatever unit of study (e.g., revision or written conventions), the qualities of good writing drive instruction.

I am not suggesting that each of the qualities be compartmentalized, but rather that teachers make maximum use of writing time to teach strategies that will help students with all their writing. If we remember to teach the writer, not the writing, we understand that it is not just one poem or essay unit that we are teaching, but skills that students must take with them forever on their writing journeys.

Let's imagine that a fifth- or sixth-grade teacher has planned for several units of study. Table 7–1 shows how the qualities of good writing might fit into each unit, providing that the teacher helps students understand that they are cumulative all year. There are many other writing lessons that belong in each unit, such as how to develop a character or write dialogue, but this table highlights only the qualities of good writing. Of course, the qualities of good writing are taught all the time, but here it is obvious where and why they can fit into certain studies.

Transferring the Qualities of Good Writing From Self-Chosen to Assigned Topics

Students who show passion for their writing are more open to learning how to improve it. This is one of the rationales behind self-chosen topics in writing workshop. However, everyone recognizes that there are times when students cannot write about topics that deeply affect them. Whether in testing situations or on long-term topic assignments, students need to write well. How can we get them to write well under those circumstances? Let's define the qualities of good writing in prompted writing and then look at how to teach them.

TABLE 7–1 Units of Study with Possible Qualities of Good Writing

Unit of Study	Time of Year	Quality of Good Writing	How the Quality Fits
Launching the writing workshop	September	Strong ideas and support for them; word choice	Early on, writing workshop teaches students to keep writers' notebooks and to develop an eye for possible topics for writing; also teaches developing a topic before writing and cultivating a love of words

TABLE 7–1 Units of Study with Possible Qualities of Good Writing (continued)

Unit of Study	Time of Year	Quality of Good Writing	How the Quality Fits
Personal narrative or memoir	October	Focus; elaboration	Teaches choosing a narrow topic and to include only information that is part of the story
Punctuation and grammar inquiry	November	Written conventions	Teaches that writers use accepted conventions to convey meaning by studying mentor texts
Feature article or editorial	December to mid-January	Voice; organization	Teaches that writers collect information and reflect enough to have a slant on it; writers decide in which order to present facts to readers and which facts to delete
Essay or book review	Mid-January to February	Sentence flow; organization	Teaches structures for longer sentences and the counterpoint between long and short ones; facts fall into categories, which helps to make organizing material easier
Test prep or writing to prompts	March	Focus; organization; conventions	Teaches students to read and respond to questions under time constraints
Poetry	April	Word choice; sentence flow	Teaches literacy devices and variety in word choices
Revision	May	All qualities based on assessment	Teaches going back to self-evaluate and choose which qualities to work on during revision
Independent writing projects	June	Integration of all qualities of good writing	Teaches putting it all together toward automaticity

Solid Ideas

Obviously, the idea for writing comes from the prompt, not the students. Therefore, teachers must hold themselves to high standards when designing prompts to be sure that they are interesting and compelling, as well as clear and age-appropriate. Assuming that a prompt is clear and well-written, the idea must be relevant and sound. This is where the students' work begins. After reading the prompt, they must interpret what it means and what is required of them. In addition, they must do the brain work of engaging with the idea to flesh it out. As writers and thinkers, there are any number of ways they might respond to a prompt. Part of the work of developing a response is figuring out how to provide solid evidence to write in support of (or to refute) the prompt.

The work students do by talking about prompts, and by more often naming what they think and say, is therefore invaluable (see Chapter 2). After extensive practice with conversation, students consider the *internal dialogues* they have when trying to respond to a prompt: What are the questions they ask themselves? What kinds of notes are most helpful? How can they decide which supporting ideas are valid and which are not? Working on solid ideas—ideas that definitely support the prompt—is critical to doing well. Ruth Culham (2003) notes that establishing solid support for ideas is part of creating strength in writing.

Teaching Students to Bring Solid Idea Development to Prompt Writing

◈ *Rehearsal:* Using a prompt, have small groups of students talk about how they would plan their writing about it. Share their responses and *name* them; for example, this group used anecdotes, this group made a list, this group referred to other stories, and so on. Students may construct knowledge by relying on knowledge they already have (Flower, 1994), although some researchers have concluded that this type of "knowledge telling" is a dead-end strategy because students do not transform their knowledge to come to new understandings (Bereiter and Scardamalia, 1987). Selecting relevant known information, deciding on genre, and writing information in order is not enough. The information students access must help them come to a new understanding through the prompted question. It also involves "setting goals, imagining readers, and considering alternative moves" (Flower, 1994, 136). Therefore, students must be shown that preparing to write to prompts requires the same process as writing to self-assigned topics.

- *Study of mentor texts:* This means both the study of exemplary student writing to determine what the writer did well *and* the study of mentor texts to determine how writers use evidence and details to support and build their ideas. Teachers choose one or two exemplary student pieces (possibly saved from previous years or written by the teacher) and teach minilessons that highlight moves the writer used to support the idea of the piece. Teachers do the same with published texts; picture books are often excellent sources for finding ways to support an idea.

- *Love of language:* From the first day of school, teachers can model their love for words by using, saving, and playing with ones they find in read-aloud books, students' independent books, and from conversations with others. This love of wonderful words gives students more ingredients to use when trying to work out how to expand an idea. If they have more words in their "banks," they have more language to frame what they are thinking (Beck, McKeown, and Kucan, 2002; Greenwood, 2004).

- *Game challenge:* Refer back to the concept of engaging with gaming (see Chapter 2) and ask students about their game playing process—clarify the rules, make some false starts, make decisions about what fits and what doesn't, decide on a strategy, and so on. Use this list of gaming concepts to model ways for students to solidify their thinking about a prompted idea.

Focus

Donald Murray (2000) says that when he writes, he searches for a "focusing line"—a line that contains the insight for him to understand what he wants to write about. It's at that moment that he knows how to proceed with his writing. Students can be taught to do this when looking for topic ideas in their writers' notebooks. Sometimes a line, a phrase, or a word will be a chrysalis—so full of meaning that a whole piece will emerge from it.

In prompted writing, however, students often root around trying to find their focus. They are not sure what to write or what the prompt is asking. Often they drift from the topic or drop in extraneous information just to make the word count. Staying on the topic is one of the first requirements of evaluating prompt writing. Even the best prompt writing that contains information about the wrong book or a war a century later will gather no points.

Ideas to Help Students Find Their Focus and Stay There

❧ *Restate the prompt:* Although this idea is not original, it's interesting how often students do not do it. They rush into writing, often because they are trying to just get it over or to beat the clock. Taking a minute or two to reread the prompt and be sure what it is asking can save many woes. It is also critical that students not jump to conclusions. A quickly written note to themselves about the focus in the top margin may help to keep them on the topic.

❧ *Rehearse:* As students go through the evidence they might include, they need to measure it against the prompt. Each bit of evidence must be judged as to whether it fits with the focus needed.

❧ *Make a story-planning line:* Show students that they can plan their writing by using a planning line to mark each point they intend to include; use it to examine whether all points, including the ending, follow the focus.

Word Choice

The statistics on young people's knowledge of vocabulary are not heartening. With the explosion of electronic media, youngsters read less today than their parents did, or literate generations before them. While they may have knowledge of technical words, they know few of the words that seem to separate literate people from those who do not read (Beck, McKeown, and Kucan, 2002). For example, they know words such as *go, push, kick*—known as playground language—but few understand words such as *facetious, ominous, conspicuous*. A major criticism of video games is that students learn few new words because when gaming they are not reading. Perhaps this is valid. For all that video games can teach students about certain habits of mind, accumulating literary vocabulary is not one of them.

Teachers must fill students' lives with wonderful words—not to look up in dictionaries and write in stilted sentences but to use and explore and delight in. In a well-meaning effort to help students understand, teachers often use the simplest language possible, which does almost nothing to expose them to new words. The drought of language can only be ameliorated by teachers who love language and words and bathe their students in them. Please notice I said *bathe*, not *drown*. Looking up fifty words in the next chapter before reading a book only kills a love of language. A gentle sprinkle of new words every day is fine; that is, the teacher uses the words while talking with the students and thrills at their attempts to "try on" the words. Clearly the matter of vocabulary instruction is complex, and the short discussion here deliberately omits issues faced by English language learners (ELLs). Nevertheless, exposure to rich language can only help students, particularly when they are not reading or hearing such words in their everyday lives.

Teaching Students to Choose Precise and Vibrant Words

❀ *Keep a word wall:* Students in every grade can choose words to go on the wall from their independent reading books, from shared texts, or from overheard conversations Talk about the words and their meanings; ask students to try to use some of them in conversations and in their writers' notebooks every day. As words become familiar, replace them with new ones. Praise students for "word dropping" when speaking and writing. Listen and read to assess student language growth and adjust your attention to it accordingly.

❀ *Read-alouds:* Every day in every grade, read from a text that has fascinating language. Include a variety of fiction and nonfiction, and stop often to mull over some of the words. Model *falling in love* for students with a moody sound of the words.

❀ *Keep lists:* Ask students to put words they love in their writers' notebooks. Teachers and students should play with words they love by thinking, talking, and writing them. For example, I love the sound of the word *tuft*, and I try to use it whenever I can, always emphasizing the *ft* at the end. Instead of picking up cat fur at home, I collect little skipping *tufts* from the polished wood or *tufts* stuck to the sofa.

❀ *Create charts:* With students' help, the charts should show continuums of meaning for common words. Often students don't know how to say they are *miffed* versus they are *furious*. Scott Greenwood (2004) recommends teaching students lots of shades of meaning for common concepts—*angry, nice, love, good, bad*, and so on. Students can refer to the charts when looking for words to substitute for common words they might simply repeat.

❀ *Model rereading:* Read notebook entries again and revise them to change words to stronger verbs and nouns; this teaches students to reread and revise their drafts to make them better.

❀ *Highlight new words:* Ask students to review their notebooks and highlight new words as they use them, which you can then use for assessment.

- *Make a list of words used:* Ask students to list words used in their responses to prompts; teach them that the words a writer chooses to use
  make the difference between a response that makes sense and one that
  falls flat from repetition or lack of clarity.

Sentence Flow

Sentence flow comes from developing an ear for the sounds and rhythms
of language. These are recreated on the page by the use of written conventions, but many students are not used to hearing long or complex
sentences. Of course, reading is the best antidote for this. Nevertheless,
students need models of how written language *sounds* when read. Most
people do not speak in long, complex sentences; they in fact often speak in
fragments! It's little wonder that students have difficulty writing more than
fragments and short, choppy bits. For written language to work together as
a unified composition, however, rhythm and cadence must come together.

Students need instruction and practice with the *system of language;* that
is, how words are put together to make sentences and how sentences make
sense. While I am not advocating grammar lessons out of context, I believe
students are robbed of a powerful tool if they are not taught how writers put
words together—music teachers would not refuse to teach young musicians
about harmony. I recommend reading the works of Constance Weaver
(1996), Mary Ehrenworth and Vicki Vinton (2005), and Edgar H. Schuster
(2003) for more information about teaching grammar in context.

Suggestions for Teaching Sentence Flow While Writing to Prompts

- *Read-alouds:* Once again, reading aloud is key to students *hearing* the
  music and rhythm of good writing. Read them well-written answers to
  prompts, even if you have to write them yourself, and linger on the
  flow of sentences. Stop to talk with them about the craft that made the
  author choose a short sentence for emphasis, or a long one to make the
  reader feel breathless. Make sure they know writers choose sentence
  length and arrangement deliberately (Ray, 1999).

- *Mentor sentence study:* Often students cannot write a variety of sentences because they just don't know how. Choose one sentence construction at a time from a book they know well (e.g., a class read-
  aloud) and put it on a chart or overhead transparency. Read it aloud
  over and over so that students get a sense for the motion of the sentence. Then ask them to change some of the words while keeping the

rhythm and same punctuation. Little by little, they will know how to write more complicated sentences without having to understand *yet* the grammar rules that make such sentences work. Students can also find mentor sentences in their own reading and try them out in notebook writing. Eventually, students will know the movement of the sentences by heart, and this will give them another tool to use when writing to prompts.

Written Conventions

Teachers often tell me that even some of their best writers refuse to use punctuation. I recall one group of sixth-grade boys who wanted to study the evolution of punctuation. They polled their classmates, considered their use of instant messaging and email, and concluded that punctuation will be extinct in five years. When I asked them what would happen to all those old folks like me who like punctuation, they thought for a moment and answered, "Well, eventually all you old guys will die off!"

Not so fast, my young friends. Written conventions may continue to evolve, but I doubt they will disappear. There is so much to each mark and nuance. In the words of Pico Iyer, "a comma can make you hear a voice break or a heart" (1996, 82). If students do not have a high regard for punctuation, it is because teachers have taught them that it is very small and insignificant—a bunch of rules you sprinkle on after you've done the meat of your writing. No. Writers write *with* the punctuation. Punctuation is *as important* as the words. It is the code that is used to direct readers on how to read the words. No directions = (means) you lose your way.

I recommend an inquiry into the uses of written conventions early in the school year (Angelillo, 2003b). Students must look at the writing of writers they love and see that the punctuation is equal to the words in conveying meaning. Let students talk about how writers use periods and commas; let them write notebook entries with lots of ellipses; let them fall in love with the semicolon. Make it clear to students that conventions are not a burden, they are a tool. Plus, they are *not* optional.

Ideas for Teaching Students About Conventions

- Look at texts with students to discover why writers use punctuation and how it helps readers understand.

- Ask students to look at punctuation in their independent reading books. Together make a chart about the meanings of various punctuation marks and use examples from books.

- Ask students to write notebook entries in which they deliberately pay attention to using punctuation to create meaning. Have them high-light places where they have made a punctuation decision and jot a note about it in the margin (e.g., "I used a dash here because I wanted to show that my thinking changed quickly").

- Teach students to reread every time they finish writing and to pay as much attention to conventions as they do to the words.

Voice

Regardless of genre, the best writing is filled with the sense of the author speaking to the reader. This sense of *voice*, which some writers call style, is what makes writing come alive. Writers achieve voice in many ways, some of which are quite subtle. Students often are able to allow their personalities to come through in editorials or memoirs; however, the writing they do to prompts is frequently voiceless—lifeless, stilted, boring.

It is true that voice is tied to the other qualities of good writing. Good writers know how to use conventions, sentence flow, and word choice to sound as if they were talking directly to readers. Students who may write with power about their love for their dogs or soccer often write like the Tin Man—all stiff and unthinking—when they write to prompts. What happens to their voices? According to Tom Romano: "Assigned topics aren't necessarily voice blockers. Teachers can make topics more malleable by leaving room for students to make topics personal and relevant within the framework of the assignment" (2004, 27). Part of the problem therefore is creating topics that students can work with. Another part of it is teaching students specific ways to get voice into their writing, in addition to the other qualities (e.g., word choice, conventions) that make for voice.

Ideas for Teaching Students About Voice

- Add short anecdotes or narratives to illustrate your point.

- Learn to control time; slow down some parts of the writing and speed other parts up.

- Describe how an emotion feels inside your body; instead of writing "I was scared," write "My mouth was dry and my hands were trembling."

- Use purposeful repetition and parallel structure ("I have a dream . . .").

- Create images with words by being specific.

- Listen to the ways your words sound together.

- Vary short and long sentences. Like this.

Organization

Some students struggle mightily with how to organize their writing. Everyone knows that disorganized writing is nearly impossible to understand. It must also be unsatisfying for the writer to write. Students can be taught organizational structures by studying mentor texts and by using occasional graphic organizers. However, be careful that some students don't become so dependent on their organizers that they cannot plan any writing without them. Students should have some quick ways to scribble plans for writing, especially when they are working against time. I find the formal outline doesn't help as much as making lists and looking for chunks of related information within the lists. Students get caught up with the outline itself, and spend more time figuring out which is Roman numeral I, section A, than actually writing. Unless a formal outline is required, I advise skipping it. Listing and looking for patterns works better for many students.

You may have noticed that I didn't mention paragraphing in the section about conventions. While indenting is certainly a writing convention, the paragraph is an organizational structure. Teaching students to see that related information goes together in chunks is preferable to getting them involved with the formalities of paragraphing. I know one young student who wrote her paper and then just went through and added backwards Ps every three sentences. True, that's an extreme example, but it demonstrates the misconceptions students have about the paragraph.

Minilessons for Teaching Students About Organizing

- Reread the prompt and decide what you know about it. Write each item on a list.

- Next to each item, check whether it fits with the prompt; cross out the ones you will not need to use.

- Using a highlighter or other indicator (e.g., stars, numbers, arrows), think of which items belong together.

- Decide which group of information should come first and why; note that in the margin.

- Rehearse a sentence that will introduce the chunk of information and make sure it makes the connection to the prompt.

- Write the chunk of information as a paragraph.

- Continue with additional information gathered together and write more paragraphs.

Elaboration

I've included this as a separate quality of good writing because I see so many students struggle with it. *Elaboration* is part of making facts come alive—again, all the qualities coming together as a whole. It is also about making parts of writing fit together by elaborating on the connections between this fact and that one, and the way they all connect to the assigned topic. Knowing how to elaborate fills in the gaps for readers, and establishes a context for answering the prompt. When students are told to "add details," they often aren't quite sure how to do that. Elaborating is a skill that will give them strategies to use for adding examples or fitting parts together.

Ideas for Teaching Students to Elaborate

- Study example texts to see how writers elaborate. For instance, Cynthia Rylant (1986) gives examples in groups of threes, Karen Hesse (1999) uses alliteration and similes for describing situations, and Deborah Wiles (2001) uses extended metaphor.

- Tell students to add in a story, a quote, or some dialogue.

- Including cause and effect is a way of elaborating. For example: "When the North went to war in 1861, it wasn't prepared to outfit an army. [*statement*] As a result, many people got rich by making low-quality products that the army needed quickly. [*elaboration*]"

- Remind them that referring to other related events or using literary allusion is acceptable.

Summary

Practicing the qualities of good writing every day in writing workshop is critical for helping young writers develop the important features of writing.

It is nearly impossible to muster good qualities under pressure if students are not used to using them regularly, no more than a baseball player can slide into base under pressure if he has not practiced it many times. The qualities of good writing must drive all the writing students do. They must have instruction based on assessment and have ample opportunity to practice in notebooks, drafts, and in response to prompts.

To Do in Classrooms

* Consider the qualities of good writing as the foundation for all writing instruction

* Include instruction on good writing qualities in every unit of study

* Decide which qualities to teach in each unit of study

* Hold students accountable for practicing in their notebooks

* Teach students to continue to use the qualities of good writing when writing to prompts

Living with an Idea

Units of Study for Writing About Assigned Topics

L ast summer, my son Mark traveled to the Midwest for a business meeting with a client. While he was there, the client invited him to a weekly meeting. As the members of the department gathered, they sat around a large oak table and settled into silence. Finally, one of them read a quote. The words seemed to vibrate in the air with wisdom, and finally one by one, they talked about the quote in light of their work for the week. Later they explained to Mark that they had been starting their department meetings for twelve years with the *same* quote. Every week they found new and deeper layers of meaning in it. Living with an idea was an alive and vibrant practice for them.

How powerful a practice and concept this is. I think about scholars and researchers who live with an idea for a long time. I think about the framed aphorisms I have in my office, and how I contemplate them almost every day (especially when I'm having trouble writing!). I think about how deep and smart we become when we live contemplating concepts every day, topics that gnaw at or nourish us while we ride the subway or wash the dishes or pay the bills: What is truth? Why does evil exist? Where is justice found?

Inquiry practices have begun to give students a sense of the depth of staying with one idea for a long time (Harste, Short, and Burke, 1995; Short, 1996; Lindfors, 1999). In some cases, the curriculum is guided by "essential questions" that drive much of the work for the year (Wiggins, 2000). Students who learn the art of inquiry have strategies for investigating any question they meet in their lives. However, in some classrooms, students jump from one idea to the next without letting an idea sink in long enough for in-depth thinking. Sometimes, schools have retreated back to skill-and-drill work in well-meaning attempts to prepare students for high-stakes testing. This type of education robs students and the future citizenship of the richness of intellectual engagement and thought. Some schools' curricula are so overfilled with information that teachers rush through days trying to pack it all in, and some teachers worry that students will get bored if they stay on one topic for too long. Yet, everyone knows that much of living requires staying power—the ability to keep a job, to stay in relationships, to care for older parents. Part of teaching should be to lead students to develop that staying power. This is not the ability to spit back facts, but to contemplate them to arrive at new understanding and, yes, even wisdom.

Video gaming shows that young people have the capacity to stay with one thing for a very long time (Gee, 2003). The design of many games requires that they be played over many days, often by restarting at a lower level or moving toward advanced levels of difficulty. For example, it often takes 80 to 100 hours, sometimes more, to "beat" a game. For all that time, generally interrupted by other activities (e.g., school, eating, sleeping, bathing), gamers keep the assignment or idea in their minds and effortlessly return to pick up where they left off. These young people are, in effect, *specialists* in gaming and deserve the chance to become specialists in writing as well. Most everyone has had the experience of becoming lost in a game or an activity or a book, emerging at some point unaware that time has passed. When lost in a book, for example, we are lost in someone else's topic; the *transaction* with the text and entrance into the mind of the author creates meaning (Rosenblatt, 1995). Students are shortchanged if they are not provided with the chance to get lost in an idea or a topic. Teachers must be less wary of boring them and remember that if they craft smart assignments, students will respond with their best thinking. Teachers lose students only when they don't do their best work.

This long-term writing unit, which for the purposes here is assigned, has great benefits for students if it is carefully framed in an open-ended way that challenges and engages them. Imagine the rich thinking, writing, and living that might come from staying with an idea (e.g., "with liberty and justice for all") for a long time. In people's lives, living with an idea is something everyone will have to do at some point: a young couple waits nine months for the birth of their child, a young person waits for years for the promotion he or she wants, a young couple saves every penny to buy their first house. It is up to teachers to model staying with a topic over time, which may require some metacognitive research of their own. The sidebar here lists some ways I stay with an idea or a topic.

When school years are planned based on units of study in writing, most students have ample opportunity to write in varied genres on topics of their choice. However, the units in this chapter are meant to lead students through the writing process with *assigned topics*. The work is engaging with someone else's idea and using thinking and writing strategies to develop the idea, draft, revise, and so on. This shift is critical because it teaches students that since they know how to write well about their own topics, they can write well about any topic.

Let's assume you've done some of the thinking and talking about a topic described in Chapters 2 and 3. This is a good foundation for this unit because it gives students a sense of what it is like to *knead* a topic to find the meaning and details inside it. If teachers hope to educate future citizens, they must teach them the challenge and joy of taking on an outside topic and musing on it. Then of course they are to respond in writing, which is what this unit describes; there are two ways to structure the unit: (1) occasions when the genre is assigned and (2) occasions when students have a choice of genre. In both instances, the topic is assigned by the teacher. The structure of the writing workshop is maintained: short, focused whole-class teaching (minilesson), small-group teaching, and individual teaching (conferring). Then, students go through all the stages of the writing process from collecting ideas to publishing.

This chapter looks at three writing units of study and the intellectual pleasure of *dwelling* with an idea over time: one for assigned topics and genre, one for assigned topics with a choice of genre, and one for other long-term studies for writing on assignment.

Staying Interested in a Topic
• I let my mind wander about it.
• I look for it everywhere—on TV, in the news, in magazines, in conversations, in public places, and so on—all day long.
• I see it in books I read and other media—movies, theater, opera, concerts, museum exhibitions, music, sermons, and so on.
• I find it in my life or in events or people I know.
• I collect hard facts about it from the library or online.
• I plan serious reading about it.
• I freewrite in my notebook and go back to reread and reflect.
• I talk to my trusted friend and I listen to her feedback and consider it to shape my thinking.
• I talk aloud about it to the air (okay, to my dog) and listen to my own voice.
• I look for patterns in my thinking and try to make connections between parts or facts.

A Unit of Study for Assigned Topics and Genres

Begin this unit by setting aside a four-to-six-week period of time in writing workshop. This is best done after the workshop format is well established so that students are comfortable with the community environment, keeping notebooks, finding their own topics, and going through the writing process from gathering entries to publication. Since teachers must establish the purpose for each unit before teaching it, be sure that students understand that this unit is unique. Their opportunities for choice are not being taken away forever, but the purpose of this unit is to teach them to apply their knowledge to specific events (e.g., testing situations).

There are two variations to this study; teachers decide which one to implement depending on their assessment of students' needs and strengths, as well as grade level. Both units have the same week-by-week structure; however, Variation 1 asks all students to write on the same topic, and Variation 2 is slightly more sophisticated because students are assigned different topics in groups. The procedure is the same, but communications in Variation 1 are whole-class and partner conversations, while in Variation 2, they are mostly in the groups. In both cases, teachers assess students' needs as they listen to them talk, confer with individual students, and read their notebooks and drafts.

The topic must be carefully crafted so that students can get "thinking mileage" from it; that is, there are some facets of it that students will immediately recognize, but there is much room for additional depth and research. Depending on the grade level, you might write a general prompt, or one that is literature- or content-specific. Be sure that if it is content-specific, the writing workshop doesn't become a time to *cover* the science curriculum. The focus is always on writing and the minilessons are always about writing. A general topic might be something that explores a social issue (e.g., bullying). A literature topic might explore a theme or character in the class read-aloud or several picture books. A content-area topic in social studies, science, math, or health should refer to something the students have studied so that they have a frame of reference for building their knowledge bank. Remember that this is a long-term project, not a testing situation for which they might have to write about something unfamiliar.

The assigned genre is a report or response to the prompt, although if you have previously taught feature article writing or editorials, you might assign those. Another variation is to let students write a story, but only if they have previously studied elements of story. In the case of a story, the prompt would have to lead to a story; that is, don't be tempted to combine history and story because, with a few exceptions for students who are avid historical fiction readers, it is unlikely that they will whip up historical fiction without studying it intensely as a genre. The same is true with science prompts—you don't want students to dream up fantastical stories about what would happen if gravity suddenly disappeared or cataclysmic stories on the disappearance of the rainforest. Don't test creativity. Focus on writing well about a topic.

A general plan for the teaching you would do during each week follows. Of course, you may have to change some of this based on the needs of your class, which you should determine through ongoing assessment.

Week One

Be sure to explain the purpose of the unit, then assign the topic to the class. You will need to teach mini-lessons on talking with partners in order to interpret what the prompt is asking, as well as how to engage with it and make it important to you (see sidebar). Here students are situating their learning. This is where some knowledge of video games might be very helpful because you can use them as an analogy. However, as noted earlier, you can use any game experience as an analogy for writing.

As James Gee notes: "Good video games involve the player in a compelling world of action and interaction, a world to which the learner has made an identity commitment, in the sense of engaging in the sort of play with identities . . ." (2003, 68). Gee also defines a number of learning principles that operate in the active learning classroom and in video games, such as self-knowledge and committed learning (68). In addition, he explains the "regime of competence" principle in which the learner has the "opportunity to operate within, but at the outer edge of, his or her resource, so that at those points things are felt as challenging but not 'undoable'" (2003, 71). Therefore, the topic should be challenging for students, but not over their heads.

In addition, Gee says that players follow a four-step process that is the key to "reflective process." They must probe the virtual world (looking around the environment), then they form a hypothesis based on their reflections while probing; they "reprobe" based on their hypothesis; they use feedback to accept or rethink the original hypothesis (2003, 90). This first week of the unit of study mirrors the actions of probing to figure out the topic and reflecting to form a hypothesis.

After extended discussion in small groups, guide students to recognize what they already know from their knowledge bank and what they don't yet understand. They can write in their writers' notebooks using a variety of entries—freewriting, questions, interesting words or facts, reflections,

Making a Topic Important

- I imagine myself in the situation, time, or emotion.

- I think about it in terms of people I know or love.

- I think about it in terms of my environment (e.g., home, school).

- I think about how it affects the earth and all people.

- I try to recall times when I felt emotions that connect to it (e.g., bullying).

- I imagine that my thinking and writing will be published on the Internet and will affect how many people think and live.

- I imagine that the world is waiting for my wisdom on it because my thinking matters.

- I consider how I can become adept at the new ideas and skills required by it.

- I think about it in other media (e.g., TV shows, magazines, books, stories I've heard).

- Using library computer catalog to find books and articles

- Interviewing experts by phone or in person

- Writing letters or emails to experts or organizations

- Using a search engine to finds websites with appropriate information

- Talking to peers to verify information

- Visiting appropriate venues (e.g., zoo, museum, computer store)

- Reflecting on facts—relevance, importance, how they fit together, patterns, categorization

- Reflecting on a growing sense of mastery of topic and using that to drive more research—intrinsic reward of good work

- Keeping and organizing notes, noting resources and citations

FIG. 8–1 *Research techniques for students*

interpretation of the prompt, related anecdotes, connects, observations, and so on—to explore their thinking about the topic. Week One ends with students beginning to research the topic or making plans for research the following week.

Week Two

Continue to muse on the topic, asking, "What do we think of it now?" Let students think imaginatively and boldly about it; sometimes they have to get wild or silly to push their thinking. From the silliness, they sometimes come to new insights. Remember this is more than a report unit of study; it is a study in practicing the intellectual work of staying with an idea and continuing to grow insights into it. To do this, sometimes it is necessary to "think out of the box"—just imagine, make outlandish connections, be silly. In some scenarios, this is actually being brave. In video games, it can save the gamer; in other games, it is called talent or brilliance.

Teach research techniques appropriate to the grade level, ranging from talking to experts to searching the library (see Fig. 8–1). Set guidelines for research; for example, require two text resources and one online resource, again depending on the grade level. Also consider how their research should *look*—index cards, notebooks, loose sheets. Cards work well because students can easily move around the facts to categorize them. Be sure to teach a research technique every day rather than just setting students loose in the library. Provide ample time for talking and sharing information. End the week by asking students to go back to their notebooks and reflect on some of the facts they have found. Model reflecting to *grow* insight rather than restate the obvious.

Week Three

The key work for this week is thinking more intensely about the topic. Based on the information students have accumulated, they talk in groups about what they are now thinking about the topic. Continuing to live with an idea can sometimes appear boring to students. They think they've "said it all" or that they have nothing more to say. I find this is often the point where they break through and invent new ways to think about the topic. It's as if they have to push themselves beyond a wall and exert mental energy in order to gain insights. When they experience this, it is exhilarating for them. You can facilitate this by allowing ample time for discussing and for them to see the topic from many perspectives, not expecting the "right" answer but original and new answers.

During this week, students also share facts, talk about their perspective on the topic, freewrite in their notebooks, and continue researching. At this point, the teacher also introduces mentor texts—that is, exemplary writing in the genre. Students need to study these texts to get a sense of what a report is, since they often think a report is a dry list of facts. Reports can have a slant (i.e., which facts the writer includes and which he or she omits and why); and they often put forward a belief, insight, or conclusion. So if a class is studying family relationships among bears, students should come to some conclusions about what this means in the larger world of animals or living creatures.

After studying mentor texts, students help the teacher write a Noticings chart that lists what they have noticed about the mentor reports. This will guide them when they write their drafts (see Fig. 8–2 for one class's chart). In addition, this week is a good opportunity to offer students multiple experiences with the topic, such as museum or zoo visits, an expert visit, exploration centers in the room, and so on. Most important is ample time to talk and write in their notebooks. Teachers continue to confer with students and read individual notebooks for ongoing assessment.

Week Four

During this week, students reflect on the information they have gathered in preparation for drafting. They talk with partners and in small groups

- The writer makes the topic interesting by using craft and voice.

- The facts are organized into groups that make sense together.

- There are sometimes quotes from experts or from books.

- The writer adds examples and sometimes a two-sentence story.

- You can tell how the writer feels about the topic from how he writes about it.

- The ending shows that the writer has figured out something new from the facts.

FIG. 8–2 *Fifth-grade class Noticings about report writing*

about the facts they have found and what they think about them. Students should be ready to interpret some of this information so that they recognize they are coming to new understandings based on new information. Minilessons for this week might include deciding which information to include in the report and which to leave out, arranging the information into categories, deciding whether more information is needed, looking at mentor texts to see what a good response should contain, and drafting clear leads that state the topic response. By the end of the week, students should each reread all their notes and then be able to draft their reports.

Week Five

This week is dedicated to revision. Sometimes this means revising an interpretation of the prompt. When working in groups, most students can create defensible responses, but sometimes a student will wander off on his or her own. In this case, the teacher will have to rein in the student's thinking during a conference.

Based on assessment of student writing, the teacher decides which revision strategies to teach (Angelillo, 2005; Lane, 1992). Usually you'll need a minilesson on matching each sentence in the drafts to the prompt to make sure they've answered it and not gone off on tangents. When in doubt, teachers can always go back to strategies taught before and reteach them with the lens of a new genre. So, for example, you might focus on some of the qualities of good writing as revision techniques in report writing, supporting the belief that everyone must write well in all genres. Students might need to revise the arrangement of their facts, remembering that the facts must not be randomly placed. Students might reread their drafts and compare them to the mentor texts, or they might consider how their use of written conventions supports their writing and then revise for clarity.

Week Six

Students' main work this week is editing, proofreading, and publishing. Teach minilessons on editing so that students understand they are now focusing on preparing their work for readers. Schedule a celebration of their final work, and plan some way for it to become public (e.g., a class bound book in the library, a database). Then spend time reflecting on what they have learned about the process of writing a report and make plans for the next unit of study. You might plan for a completely different unit, but intend to return to prompt work later; for example, including a unit on writing to prompts with testing time constraints (see Chapter 9).

> **Some Genres for Student Choice**
>
> - Interview
> - Poem or song
> - Story
> - Editorial or article
> - Picture book
> - Essay
> - Skit or dialogue
> - Memoir or personal narrative
> - Report

A Unit of Study for Assigned Topics with a Choice of Genre

This unit is slightly more advanced than the previous one because it presupposes that students are able to write independently. Much of the teaching involves engagement with the topic, but since students choose the genre in which to write, they must know the genre well or be able to figure it out using mentor texts. Clearly only independent writers can do this. You might try a variation in which you restrict the choice to genres you know the students have studied to ensure success for less independent students. For example, the assignment might be: "Write a poem, personal narrative, or feature article about bullying."

Another important factor in the unit study is the topic itself. It should be broad enough to lead to many types of responses. You certainly shouldn't contain it within social matters (e.g., bullying) but can broaden it to academic areas—ideas or themes the class has found in books, particularly the read-aloud selection. Imagine that you have read aloud the picture book *Freedom Summer* by Deborah Wiles (2001), and the class has talked about some of the book's issues, which include racial prejudice, friendship, and courage. You might use this conversation as a way to frame a topic that

Assigned topic: What is courage?

Michael – notebook entry 1/24/05

I think courage means when you have to be brave. Some people are brave all the time, like police officers and firefighters. I don't think I'm brave because I cried when my dog ran away and I get really sad that my grandpa has cancer. I think you have to grow up to get courage, but when you are a kid you don't have too much of it unless you live in a war, like kids in Iraq. You know you are grown up when you get courage, even if you are still ten.

Annamarie – notebook entry 1/24/05

Courage means being brave. I think that is it because I read about it in books. In Roll of Thunder they had courage and in The Other Side. Where I live though, we don't need that big kind of courage because no one hates us and we are safe. Maybe I need courage to go to the mall with my friends alone, but that is exciting, so it's not really courage. There has to be real danger to make a person have courage. Courage means doing brave things to save yourself and other people.

FIG. 8–3   *Sixth-grade notebook entries about assigned topic of courage*

students might consider in light of their own lives, and to which they might respond by writing poems, songs, skits, and so on.

In conducting the study, Weeks One and Two are similar to the first two weeks of the unit of study section of Chapter 7. However, you would add minilessons on trying out various genres in the writers' notebooks. This teaches students that sometimes writers attempt to write about a topic in several genres before they make a decision about which one works best. While you may have mentor texts already available in your classroom library, another part of the beginning of the study could be minilessons on how to choose a mentor text.

In Susan Valenti's sixth-grade class, she assigns this topic: "Using examples from one book you've read and your life, write about what courage means to you." It is open-ended enough that students can approach the topic in many ways. Susan has read aloud several books in which the concept of courage is prominent, including novels and picture books. She encourages students to muse in their notebooks about courage and about times when they are courageous in their own ways (see Fig. 8–3). She also asks students to try out their ideas in various genres. Michael and Annamarie each decide to write a story and a collection of poems. This choice gives them an opportunity to explore the topic in their own ways. Susan makes sure each student has chosen an appropriate mentor text and a genre before they draft (see Fig. 8–4).

Michael

Mentor author was Valerie Worth

Courage

Be brave.

Be police officers
Be firefighters.

Be brave.

The dog runs away,
The grandpa has
        Cancer.

Be brave.

War in Iraq.
Sadness in your heart.

Be brave.

Annamarie

Mentor author was Kevin Henkes

Chickenhead

"Wham!" A rock flew passed Carly's head.
"Chickenhead, chickenhead!" some boys called, laughing.
Carly ran home, crying. They called her that every day. They thought it was weird that her mother had chickens in the yard. Chickenhead, chickenhead, chickenhead.

Carly dropped her bag on the porch. She wiped her eyes with the backs of her hands and headed to the chicken house. She had painted it yellow with her cousin Emma, and they had made curtains for the windows. But the chicken house still smelled bad. When she got there, the chickens ran up to her and made clucking sounds to say hello. Carly reached down and picked up her favorite chicken, Rosy.
"Hi, Rosy," she whispered. "Rosy, Rosy, Rosy."

Rosy seemed to put her head down on Carly's shoulder and rest for a minute. Then Carly went inside to do her homework.

After dinner, her parents said they had to tell her something sad.
"It's the town," he dad said. "They just passed a law making it illegal to have chickens anymore."
Carly started to cry again. "No! They can't do that!"
""Well, they did," said her mom sadly. "We'll have to find new homes for all the chickens. They have to be gone in a month or the town will take them and kill them. Maybe Grandma can give them a home."

A month later, the chickens were all gone. Carly kissed them all good-bye, especially brown and white Rosy. She knew they would be happy with Grandma, but she was still sad.

The next day when she walked home from school, a rock whizzed by her head again.
"Chickenhead. Chickenhead, chickenhead!" the boys yelled.
"Yep, that's me," she answered. "And I'm proud of it."

FIG. 8–4 *Student selected genres based on assigned topics*

After the students do drafts, the teacher needs to assess their work to decide which revision minilessons to teach. Since students have drafted in different genres, the revision lessons cannot be genre-based (Angelillo, 2005); for example, you wouldn't teach how to revise dialogue because many students may not have written dialogues. By examining students' writing and conferring with them, you will be able to ascertain which revision strategies are best to teach the entire class. You can also decide to arrange for small-group revision instruction based on genres and needs. For example, the students who are writing stories will meet with you for revision work in one group, while the poetry students will meet in another. It is also smart to build independence by relying on students to teach one another. Having taught, for example, revision techniques for dialogue to the story group, you might ask them to pair up with poetry or nonfiction students to share their information. Then you could build on this basic information to teach small-group lessons on exactly how to use dialogue in poetry, nonfiction, and so on.

The best revision plan is to point students toward their mentor texts. Knowing how to use the texts to discover ways to strengthen their writing is one of the most valuable tools you can teach students. It gives them the keys to independence because they no longer must rely on you to tell them what to "fix." Depending on students' needs, the following are some general revision minilessons you may need to teach.

◈ Search your mentor text for one way to elaborate and try it in your draft

◈ Find some way—fact, anecdote, character response, phrase—to surprise your reader

◈ Use your mentor text to find a craft technique you like, then try it in your draft and evaluate whether it worked for you

◈ Notice how the writer ends the mentor piece; try to end yours the same way

◈ Find one way the mentor text stayed on topic (e.g., using transition words, telling a chronological story)

◈ Revise your piece to stay focused on the assignment

◈ Find a place where you revealed your thinking about the topic; now revise it to be more subtle

◈ Use your mentor text to find how writers tell us things without actually using the words

After revision, the students edit and proofread their work. Let them help you decide what kind of celebration they will have and how they will make their writing public. This is important because so often students do not believe there is an audience for assigned writing other than the teacher and no purpose other than receiving a grade. Writers write on assignment all the time; journalists, attorneys, editors, and so on write continually on assignment fully expecting their writing to be read (Murray, 2000). Experiencing the sense of writing that is going out into the world raises the bar for student writing. When writing is shared in a public way, students know there is more at stake than just the teacher's approval.

Other Long-Term Studies for Writing on Assignment

Julia Cameron writes, "If I found myself and my thoughts interesting, what might I try?" (2004, 26). "Where does this thought go?" she asks, expecting us to be like kittens with a ball of string, giving a thought "a little bat to see where it goes" (27). The act of staying with an idea teaches students self-reliance and a kind of courage—the courage it takes to put their writing on the page. It is a quiet step toward maturity to have courage to write about one's thinking on an assigned topic; students worry about whether they are "right" or if they've written enough. Teachers can help them have confidence in their work by teaching them to rely on their own stories.

One way to prepare for assigned writing on an open-ended topic is to thoroughly investigate personal stories. For example, one of the threads that runs through my life is the stories of my pets. Their ridiculous and loving antics fill my notebooks. I write about them on the right side of the double page and leave the left side blank. Inevitably, I go back to find or force meaning into those stories. In some ways, I have trained myself to find my cats in most situations—as metaphors for revision, as models for living, as examples of wisdom and curiosity. Albert Einstein once said that a real scientist "must train himself to neglect nothing, to set nothing aside as trivial, because the truth may be hidden within a considerable body of trivia" (Harris, 2002, 59).

Within the considerable amount of trivia I've recorded about my pets, there are stories of great meaning: courage, compassion, love, humor, tragedy, suspense, generosity. For young writers and thinkers, knowing that they can lean on their own stories to respond to prompts can be affirming. However, I caution that they need practice in tweaking their stories to fit different prompts. Obviously, they should not merely retell one of their stories without using it to answer the prompt. The danger is that they may neglect to read the prompt and just tell their story! Careful teaching in whole-class, small-group, and individual settings should show them how to read and interpret prompts before writing (Kiester, 2000).

This study centers on helping students identify one important story from their lives and imagine how they could view it from many different perspectives. Students begin by searching their notebooks to find an idea or story they think they can mine for deeper thinking. It may be something they've already written about, which supports some students, while others may choose a new story.

Once students have chosen the story they each want to use for the prompt, instruction moves to how to shape an idea to fit different prompts. I recommend that teachers model this by using a story from their own lives. Identify several types of questions you expect students might encounter, either in district-generated prompts or state exams. Then model how you would use your own story to respond to each. For example, I would model thinking about my pets as a way to "hook into" a prompt—that is, to figure out whether there is something about my pets I can use to answer the assignment. This requires knowing the topic very well (I know my pets well), being able to tell their stories (I tell and write about them all the time), and being able to reshape the stories to fit prompts. So it requires living with the topic a long time, talking and writing about it, and playing with it to shape different situations.

Table 8–1 shows how I might do this with my pets as the topic. Within that broad topic, I have many smaller stories I can tell. Helping students find their broad topics and the smaller stories within them can set them up to be able to answer many open-ended prompts, *if they practice* fitting their topic to the prompt.

Susan Smith tries this in her fourth-grade class. We work together to confer with students so that each can identify a broad "life topic." I use the broad topic of my pets to demonstrate and to teach students to look at the same topic from many different perspectives. Some of the topics students choose from include baseball, swimming, an older brother, video games (though this student was asked to tell the social aspects of playing, not to retell game scenarios), a parents' divorce, the relationship with a grandfather, and of course pets. After each student chooses a topic, we give them lots of time to talk and write about them with partners and in their notebooks. Then we ask them to talk and write about the topics in specific ways. Sue models her topic—sailing—in all the variations I assign her, and then I model the same with my topic—pets.

One critical point is that students' freewriting in notebooks must be thorough, as must their talking and thinking about the topics. This provides them with wide experience in playing with their ideas and many choices and ways to fit them into the prompt. However, Sue and I recognize that not every topic can fit every prompt. So, we demonstrate "inventing the truth" (Zinsser, 1998a) by borrowing a story we heard from

TABLE 8-1 Using a Familiar Personal Topic to Respond to a Prompt

Possible Open-Ended Prompts	Shaping My Topic to Respond to a Prompt
Write about a time when you had to be courageous.	I tell the story of taking my kitten Lulu to be put to sleep because she was dying of cancer.
Write about a time when you did something you are proud of.	I tell the story of being a foster parent for a guiding eyes puppy until he was ready to go to a blind person. I was proud of my work training him, but heartbroken when he left me.
You go into your grandmother's attic and see a trunk. What do you find inside?	I find photos of myself as a baby with my grandmother's dog, and I remember how he used to protect me. He wouldn't let anyone in the yard when I was playing there, and he let me ride on his back.
Your family moves to a new neighborhood. Tell how you feel and what you do to fit in.	I take my dog for a walk because she is friendly. People with dogs like to make friends with other dogs and their owners, so I know I can make friends that way. Or I volunteer at the local humane shelter.
Tell about a time when you had to stand up for something you believe in.	My friends want to annoy a stray cat by pulling its tail and hosing it, but I take the cat and hide it in my house. I do this because I believe in having respect for all living creatures.

someone, stretching the truth, or creating "what if" scenarios. We also show students that sometimes they may have to abandon their personal topic completely because it just doesn't fit the prompt. When I asked Sue to talk about the causes of the American Revolution, it was clear to everyone that her personal topic of sailing wouldn't help her. She knew she had to rely on other information to answer this prompt, partially because it was content-specific.

At one point, Sue and I pretend she cannot think of a way to fit sailing into the open-ended prompt I give her. I ask her to talk about "a time when she figured out a way out of a dangerous situation." Sue pretends she's never had trouble while sailing, but says she can imagine what would happen if a sudden storm blew up while she was out on the lake. So she invents the truth to tell the story of trying to outrun the wind and harsh rain to get back to shore. I ask her what she might say if she couldn't imagine a storm. Sue thinks a minute and then answers that her friend once ran aground on rocks while sailing one late evening and was stuck there until rescued a few hours later. Sue says she could tell that story, even though it is not hers.

She knows enough about sailing to tell the story as if it were her own. The benefit of writing about something she knows well is that she can fake it.

We ask students to try this with their personal stories. Over several days they are to practice orally and then in writing; we ask them: "How would you tell it this way? That way?" and so on. The purpose is to exercise their minds to fit stories into prompts, but it also begins to teach students that metaphor and meaning can be made through thought and reflection on life experiences.

Ways to Help Students Practice Telling Personal Stories From Different Perspectives

- Tell the suspenseful part of your story

- Tell your story as if it happened a long time ago

- Tell your story as a sad or tragic one

- Tell your story as if it happened to someone else

- Tell the part of your story that shows courage, loyalty, love, betrayal, and so on

- Tell a life lesson you learned from one part of your story

- Tell how the setting fits the story or how you could change it to fit better

- Practice some of the dialogue you might use in your story

- Think about a character in a book who had a similar trial or challenge and compare his or her experience to yours

- Use a character's experience to inform what you might do in your story

- Use your story to persuade someone to experience the same things (e.g., to get a pet, try sailing)

Ultimately, this type of thinking prepares students to begin prompt writing feeling somewhat secure, knowing they have a bag of tricks in the form of their own stories. This is really what many politicians do—they know what they want to say, and they shape their answers to fit the questions they are asked. Students read prompts to interpret what type of response is required, but rather than begin empty-handed, they have their stories to fit into the assigned writing topic.

Summary

Students benefit greatly when they see that contemplating an idea for a long time can bring new insights and perspectives to it. Teachers do them a disservice when they avoid slowing them down long enough to experience this. Units of study that require students to take on a topic and expand their thinking about it over time teach them a habit of mind that will serve them well in their lives. Practicing this with an assigned topic provides students with the opportunity to learn to live outside their own worlds and to contemplate the thinking of others.

To Do in Classrooms

- Plan a time of the year when you will do this unit in writing workshop

- Carefully select read-aloud books so that they will support students' thinking about the topic

- Craft the assigned topic carefully; make it neither too broad nor too narrow

- Know your class well and be sure all students will be able to relate to the topic

- Collect mentor texts to use or write them yourself

- Focus on the thinking skills involved in slowing learning down to find nuance and revelation between the cracks

- Practice using familiar and personal topics as building blocks for answering prompts

9

Write About This

Preparing Students for Timed Writing on Demand

Over the last year, I have talked with trusted friends and colleagues and amused family members with the topic of this book many times. We've grilled the topic on numerous occasions, talking over steaming soups and warm desserts on cold evenings, over iced tea while katydids crackled and panted, over cappuccino in crowded coffeehouses. I've scribbled and listed, chatted and mused, worried and reconsidered endless times. I've taken it with me everywhere—working in schools, while walking the dog and washing the dishes, as I ate pounds of chocolate.

But the time for imagining is over. I sit in my office facing the computer screen. It is past midnight and there is no one to talk to now—they are all asleep and, like the dog, snoring. Outside, my yard fills up with snow; inside, hot water clangs in the old pipes. I am alone. Alone with my topic and my thoughts.

What I feel now is just what students face when they take tests or must respond to any prompt. They are alone with the topic and their thoughts. Only they have the added stress of a time constraint. How difficult this is for them. How difficult it is for me! I am at my computer, and I am recalling all I do to get my mind going on a topic *quickly*. Not when I have months to noodle along with it, but when I need to write it *now* because it's cold and I want to go to bed. For youngsters who need to write it in the next forty-five minutes because the teacher or the district or the state requires it, they want to get it over so that they can go outside and play. How do we get the writing done quickly and get it done well?

Earlier in this book we looked at the processes thinkers use when they meet a task for the first time. Video games, puzzles, board games, sports, even recipes and sewing patterns all require thinkers to enter fully into the world of the game or task. The most successful play, and yes, even work, occurs when thinkers succeed at bringing full engagement to the task, losing themselves in the world of it. Many of the tasks, especially for video games, sports, and board games, require quick and immediate decisions and responses, just as is required in testing situations.

This chapter considers testing situations and looks at preparing students to compress the writing process into a short time without forgetting all they know about good writing. The sections describe the following skills that students must practice, as well as the teaching moves to support them: preparing to write by using internal dialogue, planning to write with an assessment lens, and revising before and during writing.

Preparing to Write by Using Internal Dialogue

Before students meet with the types of testing situations being considered here—classroom tests designed by teachers, district tests, and statewide writing tests—it is important that they've received many weeks and months of ongoing, rigorous writing instruction. While it seems obvious, I will say it anyway: Students must write every day for an extended amount of time if they are to do well on writing tests of any kind. Teachers sometimes say that they cannot fit writing into their schedules because there is not enough time or their students get pulled out for other instruction. If this is your situation, begin a dialogue with administrators and other academic departments to facilitate appropriate scheduling in the future. High-stakes writing tests are here to stay for the foreseeable future, therefore students must receive consistent and high-quality writing instruction every day. Plus, they need lots of practice writing, writing, writing.

By the time students face state writing tests, you will have taught them to engage with an idea the way they would in a gaming situation; now you need to teach them to compress this process. In testing situations, they obviously cannot talk with partners about their ideas. But once they have practiced dialogues with trusted partners and named the intellectual moves of figuring an idea out, they can be taught to bring that thinking to the tests. Recreating partner conversations by imagining what a partner would say, using mental bullets to think, is helpful for getting students going on a topic.

Sixth-grade teacher John Johnson is working with his class to prepare them for the spring statewide writing test. He has already done the unit of study on responding to prompts in writing workshop, and he is focusing on teaching his students to work independently within a short time frame. John assigns a topic for practice, and he and I move together around the class conferring with students to teach them. I sit beside one student, Danny, and confer with him about his work.

JANET: So Dan, tell me about the thinking work you are doing to get ready to write.

DANNY: I don't know. I wish I could talk to my partner, Mike, about it.

JANET: Why?

DANNY: Because he always gives me great ideas.

JANET: Well, can you think about some of the things Mike usually says to you to help?

DANNY: I don't know.

JANET: Try to imagine one thing right now that Mike might say to you about this topic.

DANNY: Well, he usually asks me what's the first thing we do in video games, and I say that the first thing I do is decide what kind of game I'm playing.

JANET: So you use video game analogies?

DANNY: Yes. The first thing I do is figure out what kind of game it is.

JANET: So if you remember that Mike helps you by asking you that, how can you use that on a test?

DANNY: I can think about what kind of question it is?

JANET: Yes. That's a great way to get started.

Teaching students to recreate the dialogue they might have with a partner or small group *in their minds* is an important way for them to use partner experiences to help them on a test. What are the ways they start talking about an assigned topic as if they were getting ready to play any type of game? They can use the following mental bullets to get started with a topic the same way they might get started with a game.

- Identify the type of question or game

- Figure out what you are being asked to do or accomplish

⊛ Decide what you already know about the topic or game and use similar experiences to inform the way you will work

Identify the Type of Question or Game

Recognizing the genre or type of question is the first key to getting started. According to Kiester, there are four types of questions that are asked on tests: narrative, expository, persuasive, and descriptive (2000, 28). She also suggests teaching students to identify certain words that are clues to the genre: *tell a story* for narrative, *explain* for expository, *convince* for persuasive, and *describe* for descriptive. Other important advice she gives is learn to include quotes and argue or develop whichever side of the topic you have more information for, regardless of whether you actually agree with that point of view (Kiester, 2000, 33).

To prepare students for this, have them work with their partners to identify the type of question quickly in partnerships or small groups. Come up with several types of questions and distribute different ones to the groups, asking students to identify the type and jot down their reasons for their decision. Talking and negotiating in small groups about identifying the types of questions gives students a way to talk out their confusion or misunderstanding. Of course, the teacher's work at this time is to confer with the groups and to take detailed notes, especially to aid in the planning for later small-group instruction with students who are having difficulty with the types of questions concept. Ask students to write the genre of the prompt in the margin or on the paper so that they will have it in front of them as they write. Make sure they recognize that the first thing they must do when responding to any prompt is to figure out what kind of question it is and what kind of response is required.

Figure Out What You Are Being Asked to Do or Accomplish

In another classroom, I sit beside two fifth graders, Lisa and Danielle. Their teachers have given them a topic to play around with and the girls are figuring out what to do next with it.

JANET: So tell me about the thinking work you are doing today.

LISA: Well, we think the prompt is asking us to write a story because it says, "Imagine that you woke up and found you were in a different house with people you didn't know. Tell the story of what would happen next." So we have to write a story.

DANIELLE: Yes. We have to use our imaginations.

JANET: Okay. So you've identified you need to write a story. How are you going to move on from here?

DANIELLE: *(looks at Lisa)* We don't know.

LISA: I guess we have to imagine how it would feel. And we'd have to decide if it's a fantasy story, or a horror story, like a kidnapping or something.

DANIELLE: I think it could be either one.

JANET: Which do you think the prompt is asking you to do?

LISA: *(rereads prompt)* It doesn't say. So I guess it's okay to do either one.

JANET: It's probably important to remember that they are asking for a story. So you can't just say, "It was weird" or "I was scared."

LISA: Do you mean we have to use the story elements?

DANIELLE: Oh, you mean, like write a real story?

JANET: What do you think?

LISA: Yeah, I guess that means figure out a whole story that starts with "I wake up somewhere else."

DANIELLE: So we have to think of a couple of story ideas.

JANET: Yes, that's what you need to do next.

The two girls continue to talk about stories they could write. I listen to them for a while and take notes.

One thing I notice is that Lisa refers back to stories she has already written. For example, she says, "I could write about the time my dad's car broke down late at night on vacation and I woke up in some hotel. I can write about the time I had to stay with my neighbor because my mom went to the hospital to have my brother." It occurs to me that one way to teach students to get their minds ready for prompt writing is to teach them to draw on topics they have *already explored*. Lisa is doing with writing what many gamers do with games: "Which games have I already played that are similar to this that will inform how I need to play this one?"

Let's explore Lisa's idea. Without needing to rack her brain to come up with a completely new story, especially when under time constraints, she uses familiar stories to see if any of them might fit in with the prompt. Students can be taught to practice doing this by rereading their writers' notebooks and talking in small groups or with partners about how they might take the topic and vary it to fit the prompt. They need to have several strong ideas in mind that they can draw on, whatever the prompt may be.

Imagine Lisa's possible answers to the prompt. One of them was about the time she had to stay with a neighbor because her mom went to the hospital to give birth. This is a common event for students, and many could relate to it. However, it is also something that could fit into many prompts: a time you felt alone, a time you felt frightened, a time you were excited, a time that was different, events that make someone's life change, and so on. Keeping this idea in her mind, as well as several others, might help Lisa and other students realize that they write from their bank of knowledge, not from thin air. So, in preparing them for prompt writing that you know is not going to be content-driven, ask them to play with several possible topics and to imagine how they would twist them around to fit any prompt.

You might also teach them to use class read-alouds as literary allusions or references, depending on the assigned prompt, of course. Writers who know how to allude to other literature or mention other texts in their writing create a case for their thinking and writing being solid and strong.

In many cases, the preceding solution will not suffice. Students might be required to answer a prompt that is solely content-driven or based on the theme from a book. However, you still might ask students to play with ideas: "What if they ask you about this? Or that?" And so on. For example, a student decides that the prompt is asking for a persuasive essay on the topic of global warming. She might not have any stories to tell about global warming, but can remember some information about the rainforest and the destruction of the ozone layer. Using what she knows, she imagines how she can elaborate on that information to create a persuasive response to the prompt. She also recalls seeing demonstrations on TV, so she begins her writing by adding in an anecdote about those demonstrations.

In addition, students must learn to count the number of parts to a question. Frequently, there are several parts or certain information is required. Students should number each part and include it in their plans. Then they should look back to be sure they've covered each part even before they begin to write. Once they begin writing, there is still a good chance they will forget to include a required piece of information.

The key is to teach students to muster whatever they know from their experiences and whatever they've written about in their notebooks as fodder for answering prompts. It makes sense for students to reread their notebooks right before writing to a prompt to get ideas for possible answers.

In her book *The Writer's Life*, Julia Cameron notes: "We do not go into a room all alone. We go into a room that is crowded by our own experiences; jammed to the rafters with our thoughts, feelings, friendships, gains, and losses" (2001, 62). So students do not sit for these exams alone—their lives are with them, and they can write from their experiences. Nor do they sit for them without instruction, for they have been taught all that is known about organizing and revising and proofreading their work. What teachers must do is hold students accountable for the work skills taught. Feel strong enough to say, "I know you know how to organize your writing from the beginning, because I taught you and you practiced it. I know you can do it on the test." Support and encourage your students. Believe they can do it. Then teach them how.

Decide What You Already Know About the Topic

Once students have identified the genre of the question and what they will write to answer it, they need to make a plan for their writing. Again, practice done in groups or partnerships is invaluable. Planning depends on the type of question they need to answer; for example, a story plan is different from an essay plan. So, after they have decided what type of question, what is required of them, and made notes on the number of parts to the question, they need to decide about the following points.

* What do I know about this topic?

* What past experience do I have with this topic?

* How have I handled similar prompts in the past?

* Which structure should I use for each section of my writing?

* What facts or information will I include?

These questions are analogous to gaming questions because gamers ask themselves similar ones when meeting a new game for the first time. What do I know about this game? What past experience have I had with this or similar games? How have I played similar games in the past? How will I play each section of this game? Which facts or information do I need to play the game successfully?

Surprisingly, many students seem to look at each prompt as a new experience. Teachers know, however, that they have had experiences before in other forms, whether in games of any kind, in relationships, in life. They have the capacity to transfer these experiences to the timed-prompt setting if they are taught how. Making each step explicit is one way to do this.

After students think about a topic, they should take notes. Writing without notes is bound to go off course. Teach students early on that notes are to be short—just a few words or phrases to hold a thought. Many students get sidetracked because they hear in their minds teachers' ongoing commands to write in full sentences, without understanding that every type of writing has its purpose, just as every type of move in a game or sport has its purpose. Remember, the key to writing well-organized pieces under time constraints is to think and plan efficiently. The more thorough and complete the planning, the less revision students will need to do.

Planning to Write with an Assessment Lens

In timed writing, there is little chance for revision. There is little time for writers to go back and change the structure of their writing or to rework more than a few words. What timed writing really tests is students' ability to think on their feet. Surely most writers do better when given the gift of time to go back and revise their writing from its more basic elements to the most sophisticated ones.

Students must understand how their writing is going to be assessed to plan efficiently. It makes sense that knowing how writing will be evaluated should drive what and how a writer writes. If the state writing assessment has a rubric, use it so that students become familiar with it. Also teach into it deliberately. For example, if the rubric contains an entire section on "elaboration," then teach minilessons on precise ways to elaborate when writing. The best way to do this is to study how writers elaborate; name what they do, and then teach students to use their techniques. When students are vaguely told to add details, they aren't quite sure exactly how to do it. Study what writers do, and teach that to students.

Some tests provide students with planning pages. If this is the case, be sure students are familiar with how the pages look before the test, and teach them to use the planning pages. If not, teach students to plan anyway. Even if planning is not required by the test itself, it will make all the difference for the writing they do.

For planned writing, you can teach students to plan according to the qualities of good writing model (Anderson, 2005; Culham, 2003). First, they should sketch out the ideas they have to support the topic and arrange them in a logical order. Remember to tell students that in the case of persuasive responses, they do not have to agree in principle with their answer—they will not be judged on which side of an argument they take, only on how well they make that argument.

Each of the main points in the sidebar should become a paragraph, and the elaboration for each goes inside the paragraph. Of course, paragraphing is one convention writers use to convey meaning, so if they've already organized paragraphs, their writing is clearer already. Jotting down words they want to use—whether content-specific or strong verbs—also helps move the composing along. If students have a plan and a list of words to use, the writing itself goes much quicker.

Before the date of a state or district test, give students ample opportunity to see you plan for prompts and think aloud about your planning. Then let them work in small groups and partnerships to practice planning for a variety of prompts. They do not actually have to write out these prompts yet, but they do need to have the experience of planning and discussing how effective or ineffective their plans are.

One major obstacle some students face is spending more time on planning than on writing. In fact, most teachers know some students who planned the time away and hardly had any time to write. Again, students need to practice planning, and then practice speeding the planning process up. Going from the slow and deep study in writing workshop to the crunch of timed testing is a shift students need to make; they can do it if they are used to writing. Like any skill, they will get better at writing as they practice. While providing opportunities for practice in workshops, students should continue to write in their notebooks and to reflect on the effectiveness of their planning and writing. It is not good to undermine the quality of writing workshop while preparing for tests, so keep them writing in notebooks and reflecting. To keep writing momentum going, some teachers even ask students to work on independent writing while they are practicing for the test (Cruz, 2004). Try to get students to reduce the planning portion of the writing to ten to fifteen minutes.

As shown in Fig. 9–1, I wrote "reread" and "revise" several times. While revising is a critical part of writing—the "most delicious part," Toni Morrison (1998) says—there is little time for large-scale revisions on timed tests.

- Write the type of writing in the top margin of scrap paper immediately

- Make at least two bullets (three or four for older students) and fill in possible points that fit under the assigned topic; revise

- Use arrows to elaborate on the bullets

- Decide which main points to use in writing; revise

- Use numbers or letters to put them in order; reread and revise

- Make a list of possible words or phrases to use; reread and revise

- Try out a quick beginning and a quick ending; reread and revise

- Check the plan with the prompt to see it if fits

- Write!

FIG. 9–1 *Speeding up the planning process*

Revision is a powerful tool for the writing, but it is a part of the process that they must use in a different way when writing quickly (Angelillo, 2005). There is no time to reflect and resee, just as there is little time to reflect when playing a game that requires immediate reactions and long-practiced skills. In some ways, it could be said that timed writing not only *compresses* the writing process, but it also almost *requires* that all steps in the process happen simultaneously.

Revising Before and During Writing

When students have four to six weeks to work on a writing piece, they have all the time they need to change words, sentences, paragraphs, and even their topic. Everyone knows that good writing teachers teach strategies that students should use in every writing piece, and they teach revision techniques that students can use to revise any piece of writing. In well-planned writing workshops, students have many chances to practice and play with revision strategies so that changing words or using a craft technique (Ray, 1999) becomes second nature to them.

When writing is timed, students must perform almost intuitively. They do not have the luxury of days to consider words or weeks to change a sentence here or there. They must perform and marshal all their skills to the task. Let's imagine the baseball player in spring training who spends hours and hours, perhaps days, practicing sliding into base. That player may not need that skill for every game, though surely he will need it for some games. When he does need it, it must be right there for him to use, and it will be because he's made it part of his repertoire of baseball playing strategies.

Timed writing for students is analogous to a championship game for baseball players. It's a time when they must strut their best stuff. They must lose themselves in the writing as if they were lost in a game. They must call on all they've learned and practiced in writing workshop to make their writing shine. They must remember the mentor authors they've studied and call on techniques from those authors immediately. They cannot go back to revise it all tomorrow; they must revise it *as* they plan and write. Time changes everything.

Therefore, students must understand that their writing plans must be very good, and once they've started, they are committed to them. They must pay attention to sentence fluency and word choice as they write because there may not be time to go back to them. It is also critical for them to compose using correct conventions, not only because that is one way writers convey meaning but also because there may not be time for proofreading at the end. Writers also do not compose without punctuation and sprinkle it in later—they use it as they write to convey meaning and voice (Angelillo, 2003b).

This is in fact what teachers have been teaching students all along. If they've focused on the qualities of good writing, and provided time for practice and play, students will be more confident that they can write a decent piece on the first try. This only happens, however, if students have put in their time with writing and revising. As Cameron notes: "Doing it all the time, whether or not we are in the mood, gives us ownership of our writing" (2001, 23).

Writing workshop therefore should focus on revision strategies that eventually become writing strategies. Using strong verbs may have started as a revision strategy, but eventually students learn to write using strong verbs. Yes, they may go back and change a word here and there, but there is little time for extensive revision in timed writing. The kind of thoughtful changes that writers make when not writing against the clock are not possible in forty-five minutes. I am not suggesting that good writers don't revise; on the contrary, many good writers revise numerous times. I am suggesting that some revision strategies can become composing strategies for students so that, on tests, fewer changes will be required. I wager that if Toni Morrison were required to take a timed state writing test (perish the thought), she'd write using all her skills on the one draft. Of course, there's little doubt she'd *want* to go back and revise it, because she loves her craft, but it would still be fine writing without revisions.

Summary

All the work of engaging with an idea comes together for students when they must write for a timed assignment. When students are asked to do this, they need to use a different set of skills than most writers use every day. They must be taught to compress the writing process and to use some techniques simultaneously. For example, they can be correcting conventions even as they write sentences, and good planning will facilitate sentence fluency and word choice. Students need opportunities to practice this kind of writing and to find their voices in writing workshop, just as much as they need to spend long periods of time on one piece.

To Do in Classrooms

- Use gaming analogies to teach students to create internal dialogues to engage with a timed prompt, including identifying the type of writing required and what the prompt is asking

- Teach student quick planning techniques to help them with organizing, choosing words, and elaborating

- Use the qualities of good writing as a gauge for students to measure what is required

- Teach students to revise before and while they compose

10

How'd It Go?

Assessing Writing About Assigned Topics

iving in an old house is filled with moments of delight and moments of exasperation. I dream about thanking the workers who crafted it more than a century ago: the stone exterior and fireplace, the dark wood moldings, the thick plaster walls. Their care and labor live all around us, and I imagine each stone being set in place thoughtfully and deliberately. At its best, it looks like a Thomas Kinkade painting.

Then there are the other times: when the heating and plumbing systems won't work; when the floors sigh and creak at night; when the windows rattle in their frames; when the window wells fill with water, the septic tank backs up into the cellar, and mice snuggle down into the dryer hose. So Charles, my husband, and I regularly walk around with a yellow pad making note of needed repairs—what must be done now, what can wait until next year, what we can do ourselves, and what needs professional hands.

In effect, we are constantly assessing the house to ensure it will live another hundred years. Assessment is the foundation for everything we do here, even though we might prefer to point our efforts in other directions (e.g., a hot tub, an in-ground pool). We make decisions based on needs and determine needs based on what we see through evidence and research. For everything, we know it must be done carefully and wisely.

All teaching is like this. Wise teaching decisions are based on assessing students' needs. Any work in classrooms must inform teaching, and the information teachers choose to gather reveals their beliefs about literacy (Frey and Hiebert, 2003). Believing that all students will read and write well when provided with the best teaching changes who teachers are and what they do in classrooms. Beliefs also lead to a variety of informal assessment measures that can be used to study students' work: conferences, observations, inventories, surveys, and evaluations of what they do in classrooms.

Planning for the purpose of assessment provides information, but teachers must be ready to interpret it. For example, they must not only look at students' work to assess how well they have learned what has been taught but also to assess their teaching. Many teachers find this threatening, yet it is a powerful tool for improving one's practice. In addition, they should be willing to examine more than just the products of writing; for example, the processes of writing and the thinking behind the writing. When students' thinking processes are evaluated, a great deal of information is gathered about what must be taught next in whole-class, small-group, and individual settings (Harste, Burke, and Woodward, 1994).

The end goal is for all students to write well *and* to write well to prompts. It is a known fact that they will be required to do this many, many times during their lives. Therefore, it makes sense to assess their writing, not in terms of good versus bad but rather in terms of what can be learned from it about students as thinkers. Such an evaluation shows where there are gaps and where there are successes, informing teachers about where to go next. It is the heart of reflective practice, so this chapter takes a look at assessing prompt writing based on writing processes and the qualities of good writing, assessing prompt writing based on thinking processes, and assessing prompt writing to plan additional instruction.

Assessing Prompt Writing Based on Writing Processes and the Qualities of Good Writing

Assessment must occur during each step of the writing process, as well as in the thinking processes that support writing to prompts. In writing workshops, teachers commit to ongoing assessment of how students are growing in many areas, including the following.

- Developing a sense of community

- Growing an identity as a writer

- Working independently

- Having the ability to keep a writers' notebook and to find and develop self-chosen topics

* Writing a draft, using appropriate revision strategies, editing, and proofreading

* Using a mentor text or author to learn more about writing

* Understanding and using the qualities of good writing

Although it is important to look carefully at individual student writing, teachers also need to observe small-group work and conferences as ways to assess students' ongoing development as writers (Anderson, 2000; Calkins, Hartman, and White, 2005). Essentially, they should see students growing more and more at ease using the writing processes, as well as see that their writing is getting better. Ideally, teachers see them becoming confident and resourceful writers.

Assessments of course must include students' ability to write to prompts. As already discussed, prompt writing is a reality of school and the world, so teachers must determine to what degree students are able to take the skills learned in writing workshop with them when they have to write to prompts. One way to do this is to look at how well they transfer their knowledge of the qualities of good writing from self-selected topics and genres to writing to prompts.

Chapter 7 looked at the qualities of good writing as the basic foundation for teaching writing in all units of study. Since these qualities form the backbone of writing instruction, there need to be ways to assess students' work, hold them accountable for it (see Table 10–1), and plan for additional teaching. One recommendation is for teachers to examine all units of study throughout the year to be sure that some of the good writing qualities are taught in every unit. Once a quality has been taught, students must be held accountable for it. If, for example, teachers do not insist on them using writing conventions, students misunderstand and believe the teaching is not as important as they were told it was. So, it is not inappropriate to give a student back a paper that showed little attention to conventions and request that it be edited. If shoddy work from students is accepted, they assume that shoddy work is acceptable, and that just isn't true.

In some ways, using the qualities of good writing while writing to prompts is one indicator of how well students are able to bring life experiences into their work (Jenkins, 1996). Brian Cambourne (1988) notes that students must be immersed in learning and take responsibility for it. They need demonstrations of how to do something, and expectations, as well as honest responses to their work and opportunities to practice. Providing practice time for students is important as each new quality is taught. If organizing is taught in a nonfiction writing unit, teachers should show them

TABLE 10–1 Holding Students Accountable for the Qualities of Good Writing

Ongoing Accountability Assessment	What the Teacher Might Say
During whole-class instruction	We have already studied the X and Y qualities of good writing and they are on the charts in the room. Today, I want to show you how these qualities are just as important in the new unit we are studying. [Teacher demonstrates with appropriate text.] As you write in your notebooks (or do your drafts), I want you to pay attention to one of the qualities and be sure to include it. Then, highlight it so that I can easily see where you deliberately used previous teaching in the new piece of writing.
During one-on-one instruction (conferences)	How is your writing going today in terms of the qualities of good writing? OR Can you show me where you have used X quality in the writing you are doing today? OR How are you planning to work on [for example] word choice? OR What are your plans for concentrating on one quality of good writing as you work? OR Which quality of writing do you need my help with today?
During small-group instruction (guided writing groups)	I called this group together because I've noticed, from studying your notebooks, that you are having some trouble with [for example] word choice. I know that we studied this already, so I think you need some support. We'll meet together at least three times so that I can help you transfer what you learned about word choice in the last unit to this unit.
During written evaluation	As you learn more and more about writing, I want you to understand that writing skills build on each other. Let's construct a rubric together that shows what you've learned about the qualities of good writing from one unit to the next.

that organization is also necessary in the next unit, whether personal narrative or poetry. Make the connection for them, and then give them time to practice organizing in their notebooks.

Collect notebooks often, and look for places where they have practiced qualities of writing. Ask students to flag, highlight, or otherwise mark where they've deliberately tried out good writing in their notebooks or drafts; have them indicate the quality in the margin for easier identification. Remember they are novice writers and that sometimes their attempts will seem childish. Just as novice musicians and athletes get time to play as they hone their craft, teachers must allow novice writers chances to play with writing in their notebooks.

One way to scaffold those who are having difficulty writing under time constraints is to ask them to write a contract for a topic (Anthony,

- I identified the prompt's meaning to focus my writing and did not stray from it.

- I used an organizing structure while planning my writing.

- I added notes to or revised each part of my plan before writing.

- I jotted down then used interesting, appropriate, or strong words.

- I used mentor sentences to make my writing flow.

- I added my voice through sentence flow, word choice, and use of conventions.

- My supporting ideas for the prompt were strong.

- I used correct conventions to help convey meaning.

- I proofread after writing.

FIG. 10–1 *Elements of writing that students can self-assess for the qualities of good writing*

Johnson, Mickelson, and Preece, 1991); students agree to write to the prompt within a certain, mutually agreeable time such as three days. Over successive practice periods, the time frame is shortened so that they have an opportunity to practice writing under pressure. Assessment focuses on how well students work within the shorter time constraint, measuring them within the qualities of good writing used. Students can also self-assess and make decisions about which elements of their writing to prompts they need to strengthen (see Fig. 10–1). Self-assessment, however, is not helpful enough for students who really need to improve using good writing qualities for prompts (Andrade, 1999, 2000); they must receive additional instruction based on the results of assessments.

For writing that is done to teacher-made prompts, be sure to assess only the qualities of good writing that have already been taught. Omit others from any rubrics until you teach them. Try to be as specific as possible on rubrics, and be sure students are familiar with what is required before any timed writing. Alternatively, compose rubrics with them while going through each unit of study. Obviously, the genre-specific sections of rubrics will change with each unit, but the qualities-of-writing section will remain the same from unit to unit.

Assessing Prompt Writing Based on Thinking Processes

Writing is commonly considered an act of communication, but it is more than that. It is also a symbolic act of meaning-making, a staged performance for others, and a tool for understanding (Howard and Barton, 1986, 21). When students write to prompts, they are making meaning both of the prompt and of their process for crafting a full response to it. It is a staged performance for others—in this case, for the teacher or other evaluators who will read the work. Students know that prompted writing requires a performance; they must pull together all they know about writing to create an acceptable product. Much the same as a theatrical performance or sports event, they are displaying all the study and practice they've done through their writing. Similarly, the writing is a tool for them to demonstrate their understanding of a body of knowledge or a concept. It is also a way to work out their understanding—so it is the process, as well as the product, of understanding.

This being said, teachers must not only assess the final outcome (i.e., the writing itself) but also the thinking and writing processes of the students. Clearly those who have no strategies to use to wrestle with understanding a topic, and then writing about it, need work on thinking processes, not grammar and punctuation (not yet, anyway).

> ## Checklist for Observing Student Engagement During Untimed and Timed Prompted Writing
>
> - Student settles quickly into work
> - Student reads the topic and tries to understand what is required
> - Student talks with a partner, sketches, and/or restates for clarification
> - Student rereads and begins to take notes
> - Student works on a plan for writing, including deciding on focus for writing or research
> - Student uses notebook to work on growing ideas, finding supporting details, collecting words and phrases, pushing toward new understanding
> - Student negotiates meaning—uses jots to make literary or other connections and muses on how they aid understanding
> - Student works to create conclusion before writing

Of course, it is difficult to know exactly what is going on inside students' minds; this has always been the difficulty of assessing process. Still, teachers can use several ways to ascertain the thought processes students use to engage with and develop an idea. Observation of students at work, or what Yetta Goodman (Owocki and Goodman, 2002) calls "kid-watching," provides anecdotal evidence of the ways students engage with prompted writing. While students are writing to prompts during timed and untimed events, watch them and use a checklist of skills (see sidebar). That list encompasses behaviors students need for both types of events, but you may wish to have separate rubrics to facilitate easy recording of data. In addition, listen to partnership and group conversations, remembering the following.

Observing Partner and Small-Group Conversations

- Are students using conversation to understand the prompt?

- Do students help each other clarify what the requested product is (e.g., genre, length, topic)?

- Do students practice engaging with the prompt?
- Do students value and consider each other's points?
- Are all voices in the group being heard?
- Do students take notes during and after conversations?
- Are students referring to supporting information (e.g., texts, experiences)?
- Is there a plan for students to do additional thinking or information-gathering?
- Are students negotiating to create meaning?
- Are students making a plan for writing?

What skills do students demonstrate? How might this drive instructional decisions? Where might some children benefit from small-group instruction? Would simulation of a timed prompt writing event help them?

Another way to assess process is to confer with students regularly and consistently. During conferences, ask students to talk about their process for engaging with an idea, and to indicate the *journey* of their thinking (see sidebar). If students give "teacher-pleasing" answers (e.g., "I'm making connections"), probe further to see how effectively they are using connections. Connections are wonderful ways to build understanding, but students must go beyond surface connections and use them to tie back into the text or task; connections alone are not enough (Keene and Zimmerman, 1997). Find several opening conferring lines that work best for you to get information as a window into students' thinking about prompts.

Students can also self-assess thinking processes. The metacognition of knowing what they think and why is powerful information for them. After teaching students the brain work needed for prompt writing, construct a rubric for self-assessment that contains some of the points in Figure 10–2.

According to James Paul Gee (2003), there are many learning principles within the playing of games that are critical to literacy learning. Among them are: active, critical thinking; appreciating interrelationships within and across multiple sign systems; mastering semiotic domains (i.e., sets of knowledge); taking risks; participating in extended engagement and

- I engage with the topic quickly.

- I have strategies for making connections to the topic.

- I begin an internal dialogue to look at the prompt from several perspectives.

- I imagine what my partner or the teacher would say to get me going.

- I think about knowledge I have that relates to the topic.

- I imagine ways my background can help me construct a response or understand the prompt.

- I talk back to the prompt to clarify it in my mind.

- I come to a decision about exactly what is required (including genre).

- I begin to take a stand in my mind.

- I make some quick notes and reread them to see if patterns or chunks of information emerge.

FIG. 10–2 *Elements of thinking processes students can self-assess*

practice; operating at the outer edge of resources (i.e., challenging but *doable* activities); multimodal and intuitive knowledge and meaning; understanding subsets; knowing how to solve problems; learning from nonverbal cues; transferring knowledge from one medium to another; and so on. Each of the preceding items is a way to assess how students think about prompt writing, and any or all can assist teachers in probing students' brain work as they engage with others' ideas.

The crucial thing is to recognize that thinking processes are the key to writing to prompts in various situations. Assessing students through observing, conferring, and studying their work—including notebook writing and drafts—gives teachers critical information about what students need to understand the *how* of writing, not just the *what* to write.

Assessing Prompt Writing to Plan Additional Instruction

As a teacher, I turn assessment of student work back on myself as a reflection of my work. I see how effective my teaching is by what students are able to accomplish. Such assessment pushes me intellectually and professionally; it is part of the challenge of teaching. There are no one-size-fits-all answers because students are all individual humans with talents and needs particular to each of them. It is exciting and fascinating work. It makes teaching an art.

So when I see that students cannot, for example, organize their work, I know that I have not found the right way to teach organization to this particular group of students. I have been given the opportunity to rethink, revise, and reteach. I have the professional responsibility to decide between whole-class direct instruction and small-group instruction, depending on which is needed. I also have the opportunity to differentiate instruction by challenging fluent learners and offering additional support to strugglers.

It is often tempting to rush through the early parts of the study of prompt writing. Teachers feel responsible for producing writing as evidence that they've been teaching. Cheating students out of the opportunity to practice thinking about a prompt actually produces writing that is shallow and stilted. Students cannot be expected to write thoroughly if they do not experience long and meaningful engagement with an idea. This is why a different prompt each day is not an effective method to use to begin teaching to prompts. Students need to work on the process slowly and methodically, then compress the process specifically to prepare for timed writing.

When assessing students' writing to determine which area needs additional teaching, look for evidence of your lessons (see sidebar). Lucy Calkins calls this "the footprints of your work" (1994, 196). Even if students are not writing perfect pieces (okay, I guarantee you they will not write perfect pieces), you should see that your teaching is taking effect. Ask students to mark places in their writing where they have used a specific strategy you taught. Notice which strategies they are using and which ones they are ignoring. Note strategies you need to reteach or parts of a process you tend to rush through. For example, some teachers tell me their students don't like to revise, so they don't teach revision! I suspect these teachers don't like revision themselves, but it indicates a need to learn more about how to teach it and how to teach it well. The challenge, of course, in this case is digging into something you may dislike or your students may resist; however, there can be little doubt that the most work is usually needed in the areas that are least preferred.

All good teaching sometimes requires reteaching. Use student talk and writing to help you decide where you need to reteach and your instructions will be better and more effective.

Summary

Assessment is the backbone of all teaching. It shows what students have learned and turns a mirror on teaching as well. Thorough, ongoing assessment gives teachers clear indications of where to place their teaching efforts. Student writing to prompts must be considered in light of the thinking work done to prepare for writing, the quality of the writing, and the ability to write to prompts in timed and untimed events.

To Do in Classrooms

- Construct rubrics or other tools so that students are clear about what will be assessed in their writing

- Establish ongoing assessment that includes observing, conferring, and studying students' work

- Use assessment to plan instruction

- Provide additional support for students who need it

- Teach students to use self-assessment to support their learning

Concluding Thoughts

I t's holiday time, and I am one of hundreds of parents looking for the newest must-have video game for my son. Of course, I realize that at his age he will not be heartbroken if he doesn't get it. My mission is less crazed than it was when he was younger and just had to have the latest Ninja Turtle figure. Still, I hurry from store to store looking for the game with the latest graphics and newest challenges, half enjoying the quest as much as I know he'll love it. Young people (and their playful parents) will always want games to play.

Games of all kinds are here to stay. Among their peers, students develop skills in game playing—video and otherwise—and use those skills to become masters of worlds that are virtual, imaginary, or simply fun. Too often in schools though, teachers excoriate students' game playing rather than use it to teach them critical skills. How I wish my teachers had tapped into my game expertise. I had fierce skills in street games and cards that might have shown my talent for planning ahead, strategizing, and creative thinking. Wise teachers use skills that students develop on their own to teach them what they need to learn.

The world in which we live is changing. Gone are the factory schools that were established to educate large numbers of children to obey rules and enter the workforce when very young. They are gone because the landscape of work is changing. Information grows exponentially today, and technological advances are almost obsolete within weeks of release. Corporations tell educators they need workers who can think and challenge the status quo to imagine new futures. Although schools are still charged with the work of educating young people for the continuation of democracy, more than ever what is needed is a citizenry that can think, interact, and respond wisely to global and national challenges.

It is time to recognize that students come to school with capabilities that teachers fail to tap. We must face the fact that they will not change to fit our perception of them—we must change our instruction to fit and use what they do know. Most come with a vast bank of game expertise: playground games, board games, sports games, and video games, of course. It is up to us to use that knowledge, just as we use speech and movement to teach them.

It will be years before educators make schools as interactive as gaming. We are on the right track, nevertheless, if teachers begin to use gaming skills to teach—to enter into a contract with someone else's thought or proposition, to remain with it for an extended time, and to develop increasing skill at managing one's interactions.

All writing helps humans find their voices. It helps to use one's voice in outrage or celebration or supplication. It is one way to leave marks of our lives on the world—along with the houses, gardens, and children we leave behind. How precious are the letters my husband wrote to me when in the army, all because I begged him to write. How I treasure the recipes my grandmother brought in her head from Europe and dictated to me, all because I insisted they shouldn't be lost. How many love notes and childish valentines from my children do I have saved in my nightstand, all because their teachers assigned holiday prompts.

Writing to prompts is a way of life; it is the reality of much real-world writing, so we teach it from a sense of duty. And with that sense of duty often comes a dryness and rigidity that steals the heart from writing. As writer Annie Dillard notes: "Writing . . . is like rearing children. Willpower has very little to do with it. If you have a little baby crying in the middle of the night, and if you depend only on willpower to get you out of bed to feed the baby, that baby will starve. You do it out of love" (Murray, 1990, 50).

Let's teach writing to prompts out of love, not out of duty. Let's teach it because we know students can succeed at it—they only need someone to make the connections between their outside lives and their school requirements for them. Let's teach it because we know it is a skill they need, and because the beauty and power of writing can reach across time and meaning to touch a heart or change a country. Let's teach them to love the play of writing to prompts as much as they love gaming.

Let's teach it because we love writing. Let's teach it because we love them.

References

Anderson, Carl. 2005. *Assessing Writing*. Portsmouth, NH: Heinemann.

———. 2000. *How's It Going? A Practical Guide to Conferring with Student Writers*. Portsmouth, NH: Heinemann.

Anderson, J. R. 1995. *Learning and Memory: An Integrated Approach*. New York: Wiley.

Andrade, Heidi G. 2000. "Using Rubrics to Promote Thinking and Learning." *Educational Leadership* 57 (5), 13–16.

———. 1999. "The Role of Instructional Rubrics and Self-Assessment in Learning to Write: A Smorgasbord of Findings." See ERIC # ED431029.

Angelillo, Janet. 2005. *Making Revision Matter: Strategies for Guiding Students to Focus, Organize, and Strengthen Their Writing Independently*. New York: Scholastic.

———. 2003a. *Writing About Reading: From Book Talk to Literary Essays Grades 3–8*. Portsmouth, NH: Heinemann.

———. 2003b. *A Fresh Approach to Teaching Punctuation: Helping Young Writers Use Conventions with Precision and Purpose*. New York: Scholastic.

Anthony, Robert J., Terry D. Johnson, Norma I. Mickelson, and Alison Preece. 1991. *Evaluating Literacy: A Perspective for Change*. Portsmouth, NH: Heinemann.

Atwell, Nancie. 2002. *Lessons That Change Writers*. Portsmouth, NH: Heinemann.

———. 1998. *In the Middle: New Understandings About Writing, Reading, and Learning*. 2nd ed. Portsmouth, NH: Heinemann.

Babbitt, Natalie. 1985. *Tuck Everlasting*. New York: Farrar, Straus, and Giroux.

Bargh, J. A., and Y. Schul. 1980. "On the Cognitive Benefits of Teaching." *Journal of Educational Psychology* 72, 593–604.

Bean, J. C. 2001. *Engaging Ideas: The Professor's Guide to Integrating Writing, Critical Thinking, and Active Learning in the Classroom*. San Francisco: Jossey-Bass.

Beck, Isabel L., Margaret G. McKeown, and Linda Kucan. 2002. *Robust Vocabulary Instruction: Bringing Words to Life*. New York: Guilford Press.

Bem, S. 1971. "The Role of Comprehension in Children's Problem Solving." *Developmental Psychology* 2, 351–54.

Bereiter, Carl, and Marlene Scardamalia. 1987. *The Psychology of Written Communication*. Hillsdale, NJ: Lawrence Erlbaum.

Block, Francesca Lia. 1998. *Dangerous Angels*. New York: HarperTrophy.

Bomer, Randy. 1995. *Time for Meaning: Crafting Literate Lives in Middle and High School*. Portsmouth, NH: Heinemann.

Britton, J. 1993. *Language and Learning*. 2nd ed. Portsmouth, NH: Boynton/Cook.

Bruner, Jerome. 1986. *Actual Minds, Possible Worlds*. Cambridge, MA: Harvard University Press.

———. 1966. *Toward a Theory of Instruction*. New York: W. W. Norton.

Calkins, Lucy. 2001. *The Art of Teaching Reading*. New York: Addison-Wesley.

———. 1994. *The Art of Teaching Writing*. (New ed.) Portsmouth, NH: Heinemann.

Calkins, Lucy, Amanda Hartman, and Zoe White. 2005. *One to One: The Art of Conferring with Young Writers*. Portsmouth, NH: Heinemann.

Cambourne, Brian. 1988. *The Whole Story: Natural Learning and Acquisition of Learning in the Classroom*. New York: Ashton Scholastic.

Cameron, Julia. 2004. *The Sound of Paper: Starting from Scratch*. New York: Tarcher/Penguin.

———. 2001. *The Writer's Life: Insights from The Right to Write*. New York: Penguin Putnam.

———. 2000. *The Right to Write: An Invitation and Initiation into the Writing Life*. New York: Putnam.

Carlson, S. 2002. "Can *Grand Theft Auto* Inspire Professors? Educators Say the Virtual Worlds of Video Games Help Students Think More Broadly." *Chronicle of Higher Education* 49, 31–33.

Cruz, M. Colleen. 2004. *Independent Writing: One Teacher—Thirty-Two Needs, Topics, and Plans*. Portsmouth, NH: Heinemann.

Culham, Ruth. 2003. *6 + 1 Traits of Writing: The Complete Guide (Grades 3 and Up)*. New York: Scholastic.

Daniels, Harvey. 2001. *Literature Circles: Voice and Choice in Book Clubs and Reading Groups*. Portland, ME: Stenhouse.

Davis, Judy, and Sharon Hill. 2003. *The No-Nonsense Guide to Teaching Writing*. Portsmouth, NH: Heinemann.

Dobnik, Verena. 2004, April 7. "Surgeons May Err Less by Playing Video Games." Associated Press, accessed at http://msnbc.com/id/4685909

DuFour, R., and R. Eaker. 1998. *Professional Learning Communities at Work: Best Practices for Enhancing Student Achievement*. Bloomington, IN: National Education Service.

Ehrenworth, Mary, and Vicki Vinton. 2005. *The Power of Grammar: Unconventional Approaches to the Conventions of Language*. Portsmouth, NH: Heinemann.

Emig, Janet. 1964. "The Uses of the Unconscious in Composing." In D. Goswami and M. Butler (eds.), *The Web of Meaning* (pp. 44–53). Portsmouth, NH: Boynton/Cook.

Farr, R., and M. D. Beck. 2003. "Evaluating Language Development." In James Flood, Diane Lapp, James R. Squire, and Julie M. Jensen (eds.), *Handbook of Research on Teaching the English Language Arts*. 2nd ed. (pp. 590–99). Mahwah, NJ: Lawrence Erlbaum.

Fitts, P. M. 1964. "Perceptual-Motor Skills Learning." In A. W. Melton (ed.), *Categories of Human Learning* (pp. 42–63). New York: Wiley.

Fletcher, Ralph. 2004. *Teaching Qualities of Writing*. Portsmouth, NH: Heinemann.

———. 1996. *A Writer's Notebook: Unlocking the Writer Within You*. New York: HarperTrophy.

———. 1992. *What a Writer Needs*. Portsmouth, NH: Heinemann.

Fletcher, Ralph, and Portalupi, JoAnn. 1998. *Craft Lessons: Teaching Writing K–8*. York, ME: Stenhouse.

———. 2001. *Writing Workshop: The Essential Guide*. Portsmouth, NH: Heinemann.

Flower, L. 1994. *The Construction of Negotiated Meaning: A Social Cognitive Theory of Writing*. Carbondale: Southern Illinois University Press.

Flower, L. S., and J. R. Hayes. 1981. "A Cognitive Process Theory of Writing." *College Composition and Communication* 32, 365–87.

———. 1980. "Identifying the Organization of Writing Processes." In L. W. Gregg and E. R. Steinberg (eds.). *Cognitive Processes in Writing* (pp. 3–30). Hillsdale, NJ: Lawrence Erlbaum.

Flynn, Nick, and Shirley McPhillips. 2000. *A Note Slipped Under the Door: Teaching from Poems We Love*. York, ME: Stenhouse.

Fountas, Irene C., and Gay Su Pinnell. 2001. *Guiding Readers and Writers (Grades 3–6): Teaching Comprehension, Genre, and Content Literacy*. Portsmouth, NH: Heinemann.

Frey, Nancy, and Elfrieda H. Hiebert. 2003. "Teacher-Based Assessment in Literacy Learning." In James Flood, Diane Lapp, James R. Squire, and Julie M. Jensen, eds., *Handbook of Research on Teaching the English Language Arts*. 2nd ed. (pp. 608–618). Mahwah, NJ: Lawrence Erlbaum.

Gee, James Paul. 2003. *What Video Games Have to Teach Us About Learning and Literacy*. New York: Palgrave Macmillan.

Giovanni, Nikki. 1994. In Sophie Burnham, *For Writers Only*. New York: Random House.

Golub, J., and the Committee on Classroom Practices. 1988. *Focus on Collaborative Learning*. Urbana, IL: NCTE.

Graves, Donald H. 1989. *Investigate Nonfiction*. Portsmouth, NH: Heinemann.

Greenwood, Scott C. 2004. *Words Count: Effective Vocabulary Instruction in Action*. Portsmouth, NH: Heinemann.

Harris, Bud. 2002. *Sacred Selfishness*. Maui, HI: Inner Ocean.

Harste, Jerome, Carol Burke, and V. A. Woodward. 1994. "Children's Language and World: Initial Encounters with Print." In R. B. Ruddell, M. R. Ruddell, and H. Singer (eds.), *Theoretical Models and Processes of Reading*. 4th ed. (pp. 163–189). Newark, DE: International Reading Association.

Harste, Jerome C., Kathy Gnagey Short, and Carolyn Burke. 1995. *Creating Classrooms for Authors and Inquirers*. Portsmouth, NH: Heinemann.

Harvey, Stephanie. 1998. *Nonfiction Matters: Reading, Writing and Research in Grades 3–8*. York, ME: Stenhouse.

Harwayne, Shelley. 1992. *Lasting Impressions*. Portsmouth, NH: Heinemann.

Heard, Georgia. 1989. *For the Good of the Earth and the Sun*. Portsmouth, NH: Heinemann.

Heath, Shirley Brice. 1987. "The Literate Essay: Myths and Ethnography." In J. Langer (ed.), *Language, Literacy, and Culture* (pp. 46–73). Norwood, NJ: Ablex.

Hesse, Karen. 1999. *Come On, Rain!* New York: Scholastic.

Hillocks, G., Jr. 1986. *Research on Written Composition*. Urbana, IL: ERIC Clearinghouse on Reading and Communication Skills.

Howard, Vernon A., and James H. Barton, 1986. *Thinking on Paper*. New York: Quill/William Morrow.

Iyer, Pico. 1996. "In Praise of the Humble Comma." In Judith Kitchen and Mary Paumier Jones (eds.), *In Short: A Collection of Brief Creative Nonfiction* (pp. 79–82). New York: W. W. Norton.

Jenkins, Carol B. 1999. *The Allure of Authors: Author Studies in the Elementary Classroom*. Portsmouth, NH: Heinemann.

————. 1996. *Inside the Writing Portfolio: What We Need to Know to Assess Children's Writing*. Portsmouth, NH: Heinemann.

Johnson, D., G. Maruyama, R. Johnson, D. Nelson, and L. Skon. 1981. "Effects of Cooperative, Competitive, and Individualistic Goal Structures on Achievement: A Meta-Analysis." *Psychological Bulletin* 89 (1), 47–62.

Keene, Ellin O., and Susan Zimmerman. 1997. *Mosaic of Thought: Teaching Comprehension in a Reader's Workshop*. Portsmouth, NH: Heinemann.

Kiester, Jane Bell. 2000. *Blowing Away the State Writing Tests: Four Steps to Better Scores for Teachers of All Levels*. New York: Maupin House.

Kotch, Laura, and Leslie Zackman. 1995. *The Author Studies Handbook*. New York: Scholastic.

Krashen, Stephen D. 2004. *The Power of Reading: Insights from the Research*. 2nd ed. Portsmouth, NH: Heinemann.

Lane, Barry. 1992. *After the End: Teaching and Learning Creative Revision.* Portsmouth, NH: Heinemann.

Langer, Judith. 1995. *Envisioning Literature: Literary Understanding and Literature Instruction.* New York: Teachers College Press.

Lesesne, Teri S. 2003. *Making the Match: The Right Book for the Right Reader at the Right Time, Grades 4–12.* Portland, ME: Stenhouse.

Lindfors, Judith Wells. 1999. *Children's Inquiry: Using Language to Make Sense of the World.* New York: Teachers College Press.

Lindsay, P. H., and D. A. Norman. 1977. *Human Information Processing.* New York: Academic Press.

Lowery, B. R., and F. G. Knirk. 1982. "Micro-Computer Video Games and Spatial Visualization Acquisition." *Journal of Educational Technology Systems* 7 (2), 155–66.

Lowry, Lois. 1989. *Number the Stars.* Boston: Houghton Mifflin.

MacLachlan, Patricia. 1993. *Journey.* New York: Yearling.

McLaughlin, M., and G. L. DeVoogd. 2004. *Critical Literacy: Enhancing Students' Comprehension of Text.* New York: Scholastic.

McMackin, M. C., and B. S. Siegel. 2002. *Knowing How: Researching and Writing Nonfiction 3–8.* Portland, ME: Stenhouse.

McNeil, D. 1975. *Semiotic Extension.* Hillsdale, NJ: Lawrence Erlbaum.

Meichenbaum, D. 1977. *Cognitive Behavior Modification.* New York: Plenum Press.

Mikaelson, B. 2002. *Touching Spirit Bear.* New York: HarperTrophy.

Moffett, James. 1983. "On Essaying." In P. L. Stock (ed.), *Forum: Essays on Theory and Practice in the Teaching of Writing* (pp. 170–73). Upper Montclair, NJ: Boynton/Cook.

Morrison, Toni. 1998. "Interview." In George Plimpton (ed.), *The Paris Review Interviews: Women Writers at Work* (pp. 338–75). New York: Random House.

Murray, Donald M. 2003. "How to Get the Writing Done." In Wendy Bishop (ed.), *The Subject Is Writing.* Portsmouth, NH: Boynton/Cook Heinemann.

———. 2000. *Writing to Deadline: The Journalist at Work.* Portsmouth, NH: Heinemann.

———. 1990. *Shoptalk.* Portsmouth, NH: Boynton/Cook.

Murray, Donald M. (ed.). 1985. *A Teacher Teaches Writing.* 2nd ed. Boston: Houghton Mifflin.

Nawrocki, L. H., and J. L. Winner. 1983. "Video Games: Instructional Potential and Classification." *Journal of Computer-Based Instruction* 10 (3/4), 80–82.

Newkirk, Thomas, and Patricia McClure. 1992. *Listening In: Children Talk About Books (And Other Things)* Portsmouth, NH: Heinemann.

Noden, Harry. 1999. *Image Grammar.* Portsmouth, NH: Boynton/Cook.

Norton-Meier, Lori. 2005. "Media Literacy: Joining the Video-Game Literacy Club: A Reluctant Mother Tries to Join the 'Flow.'" *Journal of Adolescent and Adult Literacy.* 48 (5) 428–33.

Owocki, Gretchen, and Yetta Goodman. 2002. *Kidwatching: Documenting Children's Literacy Development*. Portsmouth, NH: Heinemann.

Paterson, K. 1987. *Bridge to Terabithia*. New York: HarperTrophy.

Peterson, Ralph. 1992. *Life in a Crowded Place: Making a Learning Community*. Portsmouth, NH: Heinemann.

Phillips, C. A. 1995. "Home Video Game Playing in Schoolchildren: A Study of Incidence and Patterns of Play." *Journal of Adolescence* 18 (6), 687–91.

Probst, Robert E. 2004. *Response and Analysis*. 2nd ed. Portsmouth, NH: Heinemann.

Ray, Katie Wood. 1999. *Wondrous Words: Writers and Writing in the Elementary Classroom*. Urbana, IL: NCTE.

———. 2001. *The Writing Workshop: Working Through the Hard Parts (And They're All Hard Parts)*. Urbana, IL: NCTE.

Reeves, A. 2003. *Adolescents Talk About Reading: Exploring Resistance and Engagement with Text*. Vol.1. Newark, DE: International Reading Association.

Robb, Laura. 2004. *Nonfiction Writing from the Inside Out*. New York: Scholastic.

———. 2003. *Teaching Reading in Social Studies, Science, and Math*. New York: Scholastic.

Romano, Tom. 2004. *Creating Authentic Voice*. Portsmouth, NH: Heinemann.

Rosenblatt, Louise M. 1995. *Literature as Exploration*. 5th ed. New York: Modern Language Association.

Routman, R. 2000. *Conversations: Strategies for Teaching, Learning, and Evaluating*. Portsmouth, NH: Heinemann.

Rylant, Cynthia. 1986. *Night in the Country*. New York: Atheneum.

Schneider, J. J. 1997, December. *Undoing "the" Writing Process: Supporting the Idiosyncratic Strategies of Children*. Paper presented at the annual meeting of the 47th National Reading Conference, Scottsdale, AZ (see ERIC Document Reproduction Service No. ED 417 425).

Schuster, Edgar H. 2003. *Breaking the Rules: Liberating Writers Through Innovative Grammar Instruction*. Portsmouth, NH: Heinemann.

Sergiovanni, Thomas J. 1994. *Building Community in Schools*. San Francisco: Jossey-Bass.

Short, Kathy G. 1996. *Learning Together Through Inquiry*. York, ME: Stenhouse.

Sokolov, A. N. 1972. *Inner Speech and Thought*. (G. T. Onischenko, trans.) New York: Plenum Press.

Spandel, Vicki. 2000. *Creating Writers Through Six-Trait Assessment and Instruction*. Needham Heights, MA: Allyn and Bacon.

Tobin, L. 1994. "Introduction: How the Writing Process Was Born—and Other Conversion Narratives." In L. Tobin and T. Newkirk (eds.), *Taking Stock: The Writing Process Movement in the '90s* (pp. 3–11). Portsmouth, NH: Heinemann.

Vygotsky, Lev. 1986. *Thought and Language*. Cambridge: MIT Press.

———. 1978. *Mind in Society*. Cambridge: Harvard University Press.

———. 1962. *Thought and Language*. New York: Wiley.

Weaver, Constance. 1996. *Teaching Grammar in Context*. Portsmouth, NH: Heinemann.

Wells, G. 1986. *The Meaning Makers: Children Learning Language and Using Language to Learn*. Portsmouth, NH: Heinemann.

Wertsch, J. V. 1984. "The Zone of Proximal Development: Some Conceptual Issues." In B. Rogoff and J. V. Wertsch (eds.), *Children's Learning in the Zone of Proximal Development* (pp. 7–18). San Francisco: Jossey-Bass.

Wiggins, Grant. 2000. *Understanding by Design*. Upper Saddle River, NJ: Prentice Hall.

Wiles, Deborah. 2001. *Freedom Summer*. New York: Aladdin.

Wilhelm, Jeffrey. 2001. *Improving Comprehension with Think-Aloud Strategies: Modeling What Good Readers Do*. New York: Scholastic.

Zinsser, William. 1998a. *Inventing the Truth: The Art and Craft of Memoir*. Rev. ed. New York: Mariner Books.

———. 1998b. *On Writing Well: The Classic Guide to Writing Nonfiction*. 6th ed. New York: HarperPerennial.

Index

Anderson, C., 7, 9, 52, 101, 139, 146
Anderson, J. R., 21
Andrade, H. G., 148
Angelillo, J., 7, 8, 9, 10, 24, 29, 43, 55, 64, 67, 110, 122, 125, 141, 142
Anthony, R. J., 147
Assessments
    based on good writing, 145–48
    based on thinking processes, 148–51
    planned additional instruction and, 151–52
    self-, 146–48, 150
Atwell, N., 42, 59
Author studies
    assigned topics and, 66–68
    how to get the most from, 65–69
    how to organize, 66
    teaching goals, 66

Babbitt, N., 57
Bargh, J. A., 22
Barton, J. H., 149
Bean, J. C., 21–22
Beck, I. L., 106, 107
Beck, M. D., 21
Bem, S., 21
Bereiter, C., 105
Best Essays, The, 91
Block, F. L., 50
Bomer, R., 90
Book discussions, 50–57
Bridge to Terabithia (Paterson), 23
Britton, J., 20

Bruner, J., 7, 54
Burke, C., 115, 145

Calkins, L., 2, 7, 8, 9, 10, 23, 24, 28, 29, 41, 42, 52, 146, 152
Cambourne, B., 146
Cameron, J., 100, 127, 138, 142
Carlson, S., 12
Cavanaugh, V., 70
Colangelo, T., 67, 68
Content-area work, 77–99
Conversation(s)
    analysis of, 24–26
    creating structures for talking about prompts, 24–26
    edited transcript of a talk group, 43–44
    modeling (fishbowl), 22–23, 57, 78
    strategies for helping students write about, 54–55
    talking about self-selected, from writers' notebooks, 34–37
    talking about someone else's, 78–84
    talking about unfamiliar topics, 35–37
    techniques, teaching, 22–26
    thinking skills and power of, 20–22
Crupi, M. B., 5
Cruz, M. C., 140
Culham, R., 9, 101, 105, 139

Dangerous Angels (Block), 50
Daniels, H., 52
Daunis, S., 77–80, 84–87
Davis, J., 7, 9, 74
Descriptive questions, 135

Devany, A., 24–26
Devoogd, G. L., 58
Dillard, A., 155
Discussions
    from assigned topics, 51–57
    value of, 50–51
Dobnik, V., 12
Drafts, writing, 121–22
Dropick, B., 28–29
DuFour, R., 5

Eaker, R., 5
Ehrenworth, M., 101, 109
Einstein, A., 127
Elaboration, writing, 113
Engaging students, 58
Essays
    elements in, 93–94
    writing, 87–98
Expository, 135

Farr, R., 21
Fitts, P. M., 21
Fletcher, R., 2, 7, 9, 30, 67, 101, 102
Flower, L., 8, 10, 20, 105
Flynn, N., 102
Focus, 106–7
Fountas, I. C., 42, 52
Freedom Summer (Wiles), 123
Frey, N., 144

Gaming skills, benefits of, 12
Gaming strategies, teaching writing and thinking us-
    ing, 13–17, 25, 106
Gee, J. P., 80, 116, 119, 150
Giovanni, N., 4
Golub, J., 22
Goodman, Y., 149
Graves, D. H., 7, 20, 90–91
Great Gilly Hopkins, The, 67
Greenwood, S. C., 106, 108
Group(s)
    edited transcript of a talk, 43–44
    observing, 149–51
    small, 52
    use of, 17, 22

Harris, B., 127
Harste, J., 115, 145
Hartman, A., 7, 52, 146
Harvey, S., 69, 70, 74

Harwayne, S., 9
Hayes, J. R., 8, 10
Hayes, L., 22–23
Heard, G., 102
Heath, S. B., 77
Henkes, K., 67–68
Hesse, K., 113
Hiebert, E. H., 144
Hill, S., 7, 9, 74
Hillocks, G., Jr., 22
Howard, V. A., 149

Individual instruction, 52
Internal dialogue, using, 133–39
Iyer, P., 110

Jenkins, C. B., 65, 146
Johnson, D., 22
Johnson, J., 133–34
Johnson, R., 22
Johnson, T. D., 148
Journey (MacLachlan), 28

Keene, E. O., 150
Kiester, J. B., 127, 135
Knirk, F. G., 12
Kotch, L., 65
Krashen, S. D., 42
Kucan, L., 106, 107

Lane, B., 122
Langer, J., 28
Language
    See also Conversation(s)
    love of, 106
    sentence flow, 109–10
    system of, 109
    word choice, 107–9
Lehner, M. E., 29–48
Lesesne, T. S., 42
Levy, J., 59, 63
Lindfors, J. W., 115
Lindsay, P. H., 21
Literature as Exploration (Rosenblatt), 43
Long-term projects, 127–30
Long Way to Chicago, A, 67
Lowery, B. R., 12
Lowry, L., 41

MacLachlan, P., 28
Maruyama, G., 22

McClure, P., 20
McKeown, M. G., 106, 107
McLaughlin, M., 58
McMackin, M. C., 69
McNeil, D., 21
McPhillips, S., 102
Meichenbaum, D., 21
Mentor text, 29, 106, 109–10, 121
Mickelson, N. I., 148
Mikaelson, B., 24
Modeling (fishbowl), 22–23, 57, 78
Moffett, J., 90
Morrison, T., 140, 142
Murray, D. M., 2, 7, 8, 10, 21, 85, 102, 106, 127

Narratives, 135
Nawrocki, L. H., 13
Nelson, D., 22
Newkirk, T., 20
Noden, H., 101
Nonfiction genre
    examples of, 69
    teaching assigned writing for, 69–74
Nonfiction Matters (Harvey), 74
Nonfiction Writing From the Inside Out (Robb), 74
No-Nonsense Guide to Teaching Writing, The (Davis and Hill), 74
Norman, D. A., 21
Norton-Meier, L., 80
Number the Stars (Lowry), 41–42, 43, 67

Observing students, 149–51
Organizing writing, 112–13
Owocki, G., 149

Partnerships, 34
    observing, 149–51
    role of, 51–52, 133–35
    setting up, 24, 26
    writing in writers' notebooks using, 37–40
Paterson, K., 23
Perotti, Erik, 57–59
Persuasive questions, 135
Peterson, R., 8, 9, 10
Phillips, C. A., 13
Pinnell, G. S., 42, 52
Poetry, 102
Portalupi, J., 9, 67, 101
Preece, A., 148
Probst, R. E., 43, 64
Prompts

creating structures for talking about, 24–26
examples of, 21
how to get the most from, 65–69, 70, 74
open-ended, 129
responding to, 129
restating, 107
two-sided, 58
Prompt writing. *See* Writing to prompts
Punctuation, 110–11

Questions, test. *See* Test questions

Ray, K. W., 7, 8, 9, 10, 29, 56, 67, 109, 141
Read-alouds, 108, 109
Readers' notebooks, 53
    purpose and, 56
Reeves, A., 51
Rehearsal, 37, 105, 107
Research techniques, 120
Revisions, writing, 122–23, 126
    timed tests and, 140–43
River Between Us, The, 67
Robb, L., 9, 69, 74
Romano, T., 9, 53, 58, 67, 84, 88, 90, 111
Rosenblatt, L. M., 43, 58, 116
Routman, R., 24
Rylant, C., 113

Scardamalia, M., 105
Schneider, J. J., 8
Schul, Y., 22
Schuster, E. H., 109
Sentence flow, 109–10
Sergiovanni, T. J., 5
Short, K. G., 115
Siegel, B. S., 69
Skon, L., 22
Small-group instruction, 52
Smith, S., 128–30
Social studies, 84–87, 88
Sokolov, A. N., 21
Solid ideas, 105–6
Spandel, V., 101
Story elements, following, 59
Story planning, 107

Test questions
    identifying, 135–38
    knowing how a test will be evaluated and teaching
        how to respond, 139–41
    planning pages, 139

Test questions (cont.)
    planning to answer based on previous knowledge, 138–39
    revisions and, 140–43
Thinking
    conversation and, 20–22
    following lines of, 54
    gaming strategies used in teaching, 13–17, 25
    prompt writing that demonstrates, 56–57
    valuing and expanding, 34
    writing assessment and, 148–51
Time constraints, writing and, 132–43
    checklist for observing students during, 149
Tobin, L., 7
Topic(s)
    assigning, in literature class, 40–48
    author studies and assigned, 66–68
    content-area work, 77–99
    discussions from assigned, 51–57
    investigating assigned, 29–34
    nonfiction genre choices, 69–74
    purposes for assigning, 55
    social studies, 84–87, 88
    talking about self-selected, from writers' notebooks, 34–37
    talking about someone else's, 78–84
    tips for keeping interest in a, 117
    tips for making a topic important, 119
    unfamiliar, 35–37
    writing for assigned, 115–31
Touching Spirit Bear (Mikaelson), 24, 67
Tuck Everlasting (Babbitt), 57–58

Valenti, S., 124
Vinton, V., 101, 109
Voice, 111–12
Vygotsky, L., 7, 9, 21

Weaver, C., 101, 109
Wells, G., 20, 21
Wertsch, J. V., 9
What a Writer Needs (Fletcher), 102
White, Z., 7, 52, 146
Whole-class instruction, 52

Wiggins, G., 115
Wiles, D., 113, 123
Wilhelm, J., 56
Winner, J. L., 13
Woodward, V. A., 145
Word choice, 107–9
Writer's Life, The (Cameron), 138
Writers' notebooks, 30
    benefits of, 102
    partner-assigned writing in, 37–40
    talking about self-selected topics from, 34–37
Writing
    See also Assessments
    for assigned topics, 115–31
    checklist for observing students during, 149
    elaboration, 113
    focus, 106–7
    genre writing versus content, 63–64
    organizing, 112–13
    process of, 7
    punctuation, 110–11
    qualities of good, 101, 103–4
    sentence flow, 109–10
    solid ideas, 105–6
    teaching good, 101–4
    time constraints and, 132–43
    voice, 111–12
    word choice, 107–9
Writing to prompts
    defined, 6
    examples of prompts, 21
    gaming strategies used with, 13–17
    rehearsal for, 37
    relationship of writing workshops and, 9–10
    thinking and, 56–57
Writing workshop
    essay writing, 87–98
    relationship of prompt writing and, 9–10
    sources of information on, 9
    structure of, 7–9

Zackman, L., 65
Zimmerman, S., 150
Zinsser, W., 100, 128

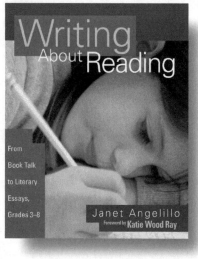